Co-authors and collaborators

Emir Adžović – Bosnia and Herzegovina

Saliha Agić – Bosnia and Herzegovina

Suad Alić – Bosnia and Herzegovina

Irena Batić – Bosnia and Herzegovina

Emina Dedić – Bosnia and Herzegovina

Elisabeth Hösli – Switzerland

Mirjana Knežević – Bosnia and Herzegovina

Dunja Lazić – Bosnia and Herzegovina

Franziska Gerster – Switzerland

Helen Lehmann – Switzerland

Sabrina Marruncheddu – Switzerland

Michel Herode – Belgium

Reto Moritzi – Switzerland

Monique Nobs – Switzerland

Michel Rapp – Germany

Valerie Shaw – Great Britain

Vedrana Spajić-Vrkaš – Croatia

Keith Sprague – Switzerland

Zoran Stojanović – Bosnia and Herzegovina

Zdravko Sunkić – Bosnia and Herzegovina

Valerie Travis – Great Britain

Kemal Velagić – Bosnia and Herzegovina

Wiltrud Weidinger – Switzerland

Teaching democracy

A collection of models for democratic citizenship
and human rights education

Editors/authors:
Rolf Gollob
Peter Krapf

Illustrations:
Peti Wiskemann

Volume VI
of
EDC/HRE Volumes I–VI
Education for democratic citizenship
and human rights in school practice
Teaching sequences, concepts, methods and models

Council of Europe Publishing

Co-ordination for production, design and editing of this volume was carried out by IPE (International Projects in Education, www.phzh.ch/ipe) of the Zurich University of Teacher Education (Pädagogische Hochschule Zürich – PHZH).

This publication was co-financed by the Swiss Agency for Development and Cooperation (SDC).

pädagogische hochschule zürich

International Projects in Education
Transferzentrum für internationale Bildungsprojekte

Schweizerische Eidgenossenschaft
Confédération suisse
Confederazione Svizzera
Confederaziun svizra

Swiss Agency for Development and Cooperation SDC

Text proofread by the Documents and Publications Production Department (DPPD), Council of Europe
Illustrations: Peti Wiskemann
Cover: Peti Wiskemann
Layout: Ogham/Mourreau

Council of Europe Publishing
F-67075 Strasbourg Cedex
http://book.coe.int

ISBN 928-92-871-6332-5
© Council of Europe, December 2008
Printed in Belgium

Contents

Chapter 5 – Making justice work

Chapter 6 – Understanding political philosophy

Chapter 7 – Taking part in politics

Chapter 8 – Dealing with conflict

Illustrations

Introduction

1. What this book has to offer

This book contains a collection of 47 exercises and models for Education for Democratic Citizenship (EDC) and Human Rights Education (HRE) in schools and also in informal settings of education. These teaching models provide the framework to activate students, and they offer examples and inroads into understanding general principles of democracy and human rights (inductive approach, teaching by example).

The user will find that many of these teaching models require few and simple resources (low budget principle).

In a lesson or unit, preferably not more than four lessons, these models need to be embedded within a context, usually following a three-step structure:

1. The lesson or unit begins with an introduction to clarify the topic of the lesson, its purpose and objectives. The students become interested in the topic.

2. The students receive instructions on how to carry out the exercise and the necessary materials. They then become engaged in their activity.

3. This is a phase of careful reflection, discussion and instruction. Common methods are student feedback, classroom discussion, critical thinking and instruction by the teacher to introduce the key concept underlying the model. Without this third phase, the students will gain the impression they are simply playing a game for its own sake.

Phases 1 and 3 are not included in the presentation of the models (phase 2). The introductions to the chapters provide a briefing on the key concept or issue that is the focus of the exercises in that section; here, support can be found for phase 3. The target group of this book is the more experienced teacher and the teacher who is willing to spend some time preparing the lesson carefully. Preparation is primarily a task of careful thinking, focusing on phase 3. What feedback will my students give me? What feelings will this exercise arouse? What is the key concept that my students should be able to understand? How do I intend to introduce it? How can it be applied afterwards?

Which questions a teacher chooses and how he or she answers them will vary, depending on the specific group of learners, their age and cultural background. We have described examples of how to implement some of the models in this book in the companion volumes of this EDC/HRE edition.

Many exercises are adaptable for different age groups, as the level of reflection may vary. Some models, however, are more complex and abstract than others and therefore more suitable for more advanced students.

2. The shared European approach to EDC/HRE

The user will discover that the models follow different approaches of teaching and learning. Some focus more on creating an authentic experience (e.g. "A bouquet of flowers", or "The jigsaw puzzle"), others emphasise student activity in a role-play setting (e.g. "The tourists"). There is a third category of materials that focuses on specific topics and is more material based (e.g. "Basic concepts of political thought"). Finally, there are designs for project work leading to a product (e.g. "The human rights poster").

The wide variety of approaches reflects the fact that authors from all parts of Europe have contributed to this book. They have drawn on different sources and traditions of teaching and learning, and have selected models that they know from practical experience and testing in class.

However, there is a shared understanding of EDC/HRE that permeates every part of this book: in EDC/HRE, the method carries the message. Teaching *about* democracy and human rights must be reflected by teaching in the spirit of these principles, that is, teaching *through* democracy and human rights. Therefore these models follow the principle of task-based learning and learning by personal experience. This shared understanding of EDC/HRE may truly be called the *European approach*.

The original version of this book was produced to support the teacher training seminars for EDC/HRE in Bosnia and Herzegovina after the war (1992-95). The Council of Europe arranged seminars for teachers from 1996 and these activities continued until 2006. The objective of these seminars was to support the peace-building process after the war. EDC/HRE should encourage the young generation to develop a political culture that supports a modern pluralist and tolerant society with firmly established democratic institutions.

In the first two years, the authors of this book were brought together to train teachers across Bosnia and Herzegovina in summer seminars lasting for up to two weeks. We found that the teachers were highly interested and willing to rise to the challenge of educating their students in democracy and human rights. However, they urgently requested materials to guide and support them in their work. Within a year, the first edition of this book was produced. It soon became known as the "Blue Folder", because of its link to the Council of Europe, and was widely used, not only by teachers in Bosnia and Herzegovina, but also in other countries including the Russian Federation, Moldova, Croatia, Serbia and Montenegro. The feedback from these users contributed to an improved edition in 2000. We found that many teachers required guidance and support in task-based learning and integrating task-based and conceptual learning, as outlined by the three-step model above.

We responded by developing teaching models that describe the steps within a four-lesson sequence in detail. Revised versions of these models are to be found in volumes III, IV and V of this EDC/HRE series.

This edition of teaching models in EDC/HRE no longer refers to the specific context of Bosnia and Herzegovina. As the teaching models represent the shared European approach to EDC and HRE, they may also be used throughout Europe and, for that matter, also in other parts of the world. The different authors are united in a choir, as it were, singing the same piece, but with their distinctive voices. This offers users the chance to select and to try out different approaches and traditions within the European approach to EDC and HRE.

Acknowledgements

We wish to thank all the authors who contributed to this book and gave it its wealth of ideas and approaches. We also express our gratitude to the teachers, pedagogical advisers, trainers and the members of the portfolio assessment team in Bosnia and Herzegovina, who tested the models and gave us valuable feedback. We thank Ms Olöf Olafsdottir and Ms Sarah Keating-Chetwynd from the Council of Europe for their patience, encouragement and support in seeing this project through. The SDC (Swiss Agency for Development and Co-operation, Bern) gave a generous contribution that enabled IPE (International Projects in Education), an institute of PHZH (Zurich University of Teacher Education), to monitor the project. And finally, our special thanks go to Mr Emir Adžović, Council of Europe, Sarajevo, for his unwavering support in all those teacher training seminars in Goražde, Brčko, Sarajevo, Banja Luka and elsewhere, in which we introduced the "Blue Folder" and received the feedback that went into the production of this new revised version.

Zurich and Weingarten, July 2008

Rolf Gollob

Peter Krapf

Chapter 1 –
Building up classroom atmosphere

Introduction

The picture shows students working in the classroom. To the left, a boy and a girl are working together, their materials, including a globe, on the table. They seem to be engaged in discussion. In the background, a student or perhaps a teacher is giving a presentation. The girl to the right has her hand raised waiting to be called. Everyone in class is working hard and seems to be enjoying it. Classroom atmosphere is crucial for effective work and learning.

These five exercises focus on how to create, or restore, an atmosphere in class that allows students to feel comfortable and safe. This basic requirement supports efficiency of teaching and learning, as disruptions invariably take priority and consume time and energy.

EDC/HRE has much in common with good teaching. This does not only apply to these five models, but to all the exercises in this book.

These models have not, however, primarily been conceived as tools of class management; they carry a deeper, more meaningful message. Educational reform today is, to a considerable extent, an issue of how to move forward from delivering a fixed, seemingly timeless set of knowledge and insights towards a more dynamic concept of lifelong learning that requires competence building rather than the accumulation of facts and figures. From this perspective, school is conceived as a micro-society – a place where students encounter experiences and problems that have much in common with adult life. Students should therefore learn how to deal with such problems in school. These exercises help students to make their micro-society work by getting to know others, agreeing on rules within a group, sharing personal experience with others and building self-esteem, defining one's own identity within a group and co-operating with others. These tasks are equally important and suitable for young and older students, but the level of reflection will vary.

Finally, in terms of EDC/HRE, these exercises carry a clear message of teaching *through* or *in* the spirit of democracy and human rights. Each student is an individual who contributes something personal and special to the community of students and teachers in class. Each student should be treated with interest and respect. Every rule should be applied equally to everyone. This means: "What I expect from others they may expect from me." The students should be made aware of this message, so reflection and critical thinking in class are essential.

Exercise 1.1. – Matching cards

Educational objective	This exercise enables students to make contact with others in a non-threatening way.
Note on use	Teachers can use this exercise to assess the learning needs and expectations of their student group.
Resources	A set of cards that form pairs.

Procedure

1.   The teacher gives out the cards randomly and asks the students to find their other half.

2.   When they have found each other, the students spend 5-10 minutes finding out some basic information about each other:

   – their name

   – their family

   – where they live

   – their favourite animal or pop group or football team or colour, etc.

3.   The students return to the plenary. Each student has the opportunity to briefly introduce their partner to the rest of the group.[1]

4.   The students are seated in a circle of chairs. In order to generate some feedback, the teacher encourages the students to comment on what was new to them or what struck them in particular.

Extension

This activity can be developed further by asking, at primary school level for example, all those students whose favourite colour is red to get together, so that small discussion groups can be formed.

Variation

The students explore different ways of presenting their information, for instance through mime, by making a poster "advertising" their partner or by writing a poem.

Materials

A set of cards on which is written and drawn an object which has a partner on another card.

The cards should show writing and pictures which will enable younger students and those with learning difficulties to take full part in the exercise.

rose – thorn	day – night	knife – fork	shoe – sock
light – dark	salt – pepper	pen – paper	table – chair
hot – cold	high – low	strong – weak	up – down
on – off	open – closed	big – small	fast – slow
clean – dirty	rough – smooth	stop – go	start – finish
good – bad	yes – no	friend – enemy	fat – thin
sun – moon	brother – sister	boy – girl	

1. This needs to be explained when introducing the exercise so that students can choose how much they want to disclose about themselves.

Exercise 1.2. – Rights, responsibilities and rules in the classroom

Educational objectives	This activity introduces a "step-by-step" approach to use with students in order to establish democratically agreed rules for their class group.
	The students experience that their contribution matters and that they have a chance to influence the drafting of the rules. They develop a sense of "ownership" and experience active participation in the setting of the class community as a micro-society.
	The students become aware of links between rights, responsibilities and rules (standing for laws in the classroom context).
Resources	Large sheets of paper divided into three equal parts.

Procedure

1. Using a group-forming "game" (e.g. by handing out matching cards to form groups of jugglers, violinists, etc.) the class is divided into three, six, or nine groups depending on the class size. There should be no more than five students in each group. Each group is either A, B or C.

2. Each group appoints a spokesperson. The teacher asks the groups for brief feedback – how did they choose their spokesperson?

3. Each group has a sheet of paper divided into three. Using the top third of the paper, they record what they believe to be the rights of every individual (including the teacher) in their class. They should record every suggestion and each suggestion should be numbered.

4. The students give feedback, guided by the following questions. How well do you think you have completed the task? What were you all doing that helped? What hindered?

5. The students pass their work on to the next group (A to B, B to C, C to A).

6. Each group considers the list of rights generated by the previous group, guided by the following questions. What responsibilities do we have in order to respect those rights? What do we need to do? How do we need to behave? For example: "Everyone has the right to be heard." – "We have a responsibility to listen."

    Using the same numbers as used in the rights section, the students write down a corresponding responsibility (if they can think of one) in the middle third of the paper.[2]

7. Teacher input: rules for rules.

    – Decide on a few rules that will be prominently displayed in the classroom.

    – They should be positively phrased – DO something rather than DON'T do something.

    – They must be specific and describe the required behaviour, e.g. the right to be heard; we have a *responsibility* to listen; *rule* – remain silent when others are speaking.

8. The students pass their sheet of paper on once again. The groups consider all the information from the previous two groups and agree on a maximum of five rules. These are written in bold letters on the final third of the paper. This set of rules is detached and stuck on a wall. Each group's spokesperson explains their rules to the whole class.

    Teacher-led discussion. The students identify redundant rules and agree which duplicate(s) can be deleted. Some groups may not be willing to allow their submission to be deleted,

---

2. Students sometimes find it difficult to find a responsibility for every right.

while others may. The students should try to reach a decision that everyone agrees to. Rather than excluding a group's work, duplicates can be retained for further consideration.

9. Voting for the rules. Each student has four tokens to "spend" on the rules that they believe should be included in their classroom. They can cast their vote by allocating their tokens in any way they wish; for example they may wish to cast all of their votes for one rule or spread them evenly. The four rules with the highest number of votes cast become the rules for their classroom. They can be written up, signed by each student and displayed prominently in the classroom.

10. Reflection. What helped/hindered? How did you contribute to the activities? Did you notice anyone else in the class who did things that helped? What did they do?

    This is the first opportunity for the class to apply their rules and to reinforce them. The teacher could praise those students who are respecting the rules. If at all possible the teacher should ignore those who are not, otherwise it provides them with "the limelight" for negative reasons.

Exercise 1.3. – Identity coat of arms

Educational objectives	Enhancement of self-esteem; individuals are encouraged to recognise and celebrate positive aspects of themselves.
	Groups find their common goals.
Note on use	This exercise allows the students to become actively involved very quickly. It is ideal in a newly set up learning group or at the beginning of a training session.
Resources	Coat of arms poster for each group of students, coloured pens or pencils, pictures from magazines, etc.

Procedure

1. Using a group-forming "game" (e.g. by handing out matching cards to form groups of jugglers, violinists, etc.) the class is divided into three, six, or nine groups depending on the class size. There should be no more than five students in each group. Each group is either A, B or C.

1. The students work in groups of four. Each student is given an outline of a coat of arms, which is divided into four sections and has a scroll beneath it. The parts may already be cut out from a second copy so that they can be glued on the main coat when finished.

2. Task:

    Individual preparation:

    – take notes answering the following questions:

    - How do you perceive yourself?

    - What do you need?

    - What are you capable of doing?

    - What do you regret when you think about your own life?

    – draw (or select) a symbol or symbols that represent your notes (colours, coloured paper, magazine pictures, etc.).

    Group work:

    – explain your symbol(s) to your group members

    – glue all parts on your coat of arms

    – find a common symbol for your group (centre), a motto for your ideas (top flag) and a name for your group (bottom flag).

3. The completed coats of arms are presented by a group member to the plenary and are displayed alongside everyone else's on the wall.

Materials

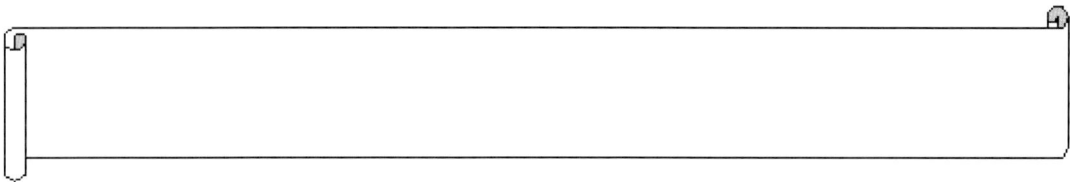

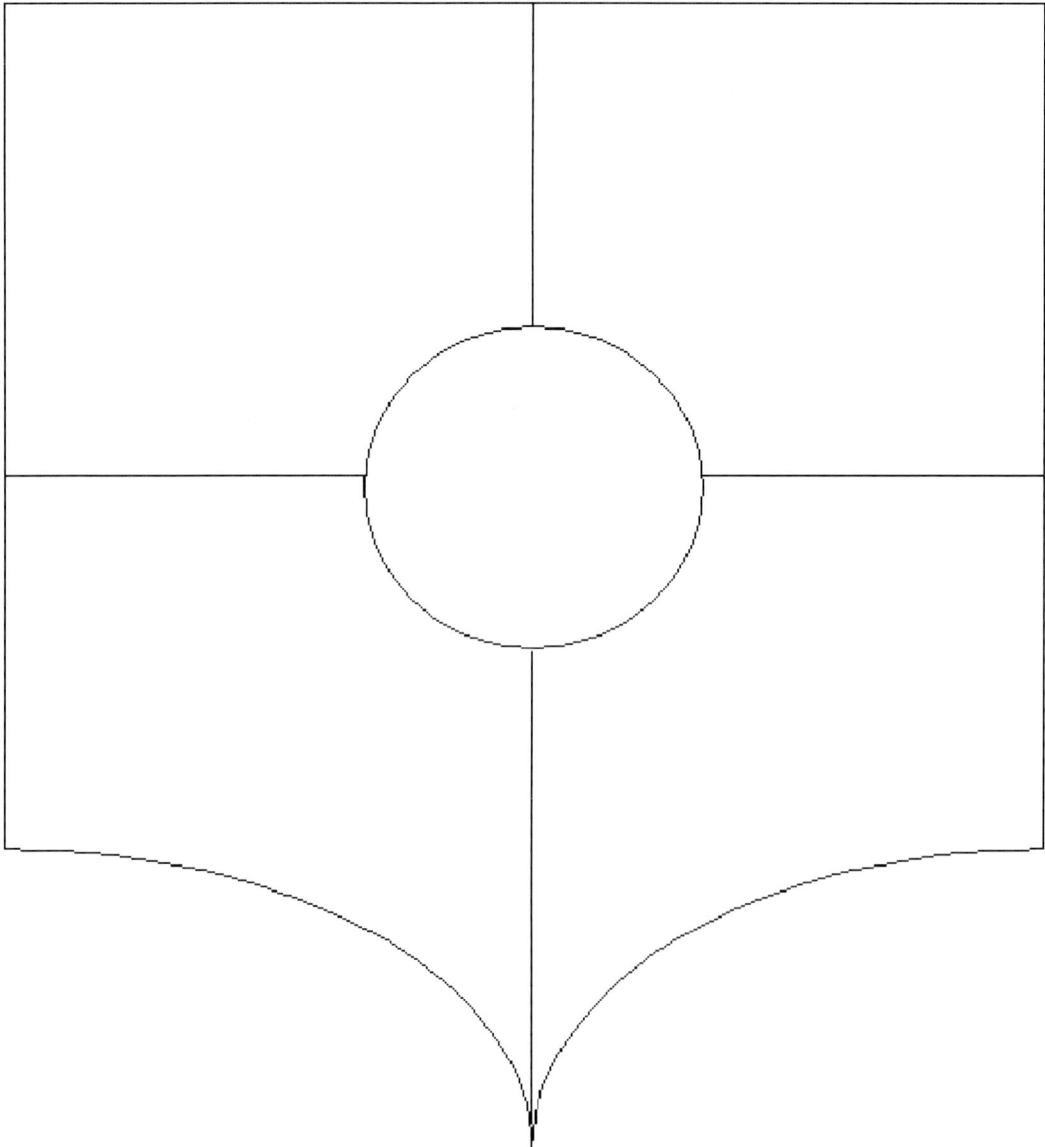

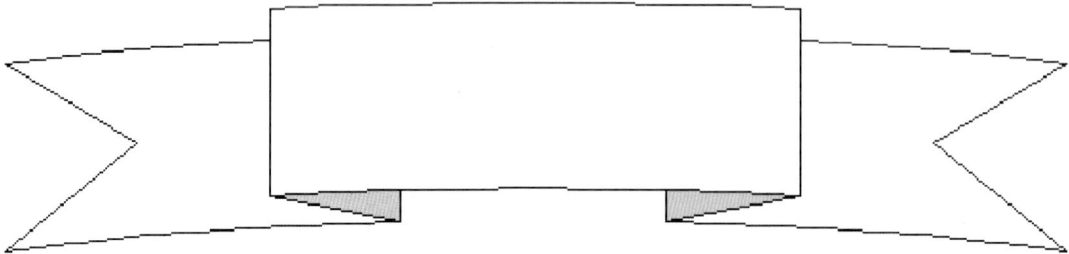

Exercice 1.4. – A bouquet of flowers

Educational objectives	The objective of the exercise is to support group cohesion and enhance self-esteem.
	The students appreciate that individuals in a group are unique and different, but also contribute to the overall strength of the group.
Resources	A small portrait photograph of the student no bigger than 3 cm square (a drawn self-portrait is possible too).
	Yellow or orange paper cut into round pieces of approximately 6 cm diameter to create the centre of the flower.
	Paper in bright colours cut into the shape of petals, coloured ribbon, if at hand, markers or pencils in several colours, two large sheets of flipchart size paper, glue or other adhesive.

Procedure

1.   Each student has a round piece of paper onto which they stick their photograph.

2.   Each student takes six petals and on each writes one or two positive words about:

- what a teacher might say about them

- what a male member of their family might say about them

- what a female member of their family might say about them

- what they say about themselves

- what a friend might say about them

- what somebody else in the room, school or community might say about them.

3.   The student pastes the petals around the edge of the photograph to create a flower head.

4.   The teacher or the students arrange each flower head on the display paper.

5.   The teacher or the students draw the stems and leaves of each flower to create a bouquet. Attaching a bow of ribbon makes the bouquet look very special!

Extension

Sitting in a circle, the students give their comments. This helps the students to understand the symbolic meaning: the bouquet would lose its beauty if some flowers were missing (community); each flower is different and adds something unique (dignity of person); at the same time, all flowers are similar and therefore one is as important as the other (equality). The concepts in brackets may be included in classes with older students.

Exercice 1.5. – Chinese sticks

Educational objectives	The students are trained in the skills of team players. They experience what it means to have to depend on others, and others having to depend on them (interdependence).
Resources	Chinese sticks or pencils, biros, etc. (approximately 15 cm long).

Procedure

1. The class is divided into groups of about eight students. The groups are told that they are to cover a certain distance (if possible, the exercise should be done outside the school building).

2. The groups stand in lines, with a distance of about 1-1.5 metres between them.

3. The students take their Chinese sticks (or biros, pencils) between the tips of their forefingers. The sticks now link the students together.

4. Now the groups must race to a goal that has been set beforehand, for example the classroom or the other end of the schoolyard. If two students drop their stick, the whole team must return to the starting point and begin again from there. The teams are free to develop the best technique and strategy to move swiftly to the goal without dropping the sticks.

   Depending on how difficult the task proves to be for the students, these rules can be applied more or less strictly.

Extension

1. Some students can act as external observers who can comment on the way the groups co-operated with each other.

2. The activities can be filmed to show different forms of behaviour.

Chapter 2 – Clarifying values

Introduction

In modern society, we may – and we must – choose the values that we think are important and meaningful for us. In making such choices, we are using our freedom of person, thought and belief and also our freedom of expression when we confess to our views in public. Therefore the exercises in this chapter address a key principle of human rights – the freedom of person or the individual.

As the illustration shows, however, personal freedom comes with the need to make choices. Free people can be very lonely people. No one can, or should, tell us what to believe in or what values we should choose. And we must make a choice – or how else would we know what is important in life? Choosing values is therefore a key issue for young people in their effort to answer the question: Who am I? What is my identity?

From a different point of view, from the needs of society as a whole, we find that freedom of the individual will lead to a pluralistic society, with its members adhering to different values and beliefs. Pluralism can be a source of conflict. This gives rise to the question as to which values our community and our democracy rely on, for example appreciation of compromise, non-violence or integration of minorities. As a rule, if the members of a society succeed in agreeing on the rules of peaceful, non-violent argument and decision making, they can deal with a lot of controversy in their views and interests.

All these questions are equally important in the micro-society of a school class and in society as a whole. In a democratic community, no individual or authority has the right to define values for all. Rather, citizens will negotiate a minimum agreement on certain values. Therefore it is not the teacher's business to define values in terms of political correctness or a particular party, belief or ideology. The students need to learn how to make use of their freedom of thought and how to share their choices with others.

These exercises support the students by developing their skills of negotiation. They become aware of the fundamental principle of reversibility. They understand that our choice of values has a lot to do with our social situation and our interests. In every exercise, how the students argue – peacefully and in mutual respect – is just as important as what they actually argue in favour of or against.

Exercise 2.1. – The raft game

Educational objectives	The students are introduced to the notion of values.
	The students learn how to identify prejudices.
Resources	Cards giving information about characters.

Procedure

Nine people are adrift on a raft in the open sea. They do not know their exact position. The raft is too small for all of them. Four of them must be thrown into the sea.

Who will they be and why?

Each student receives a card giving some information about the character that she or he is to represent.

This is not only a role-play but also a matter of identifying with a character by finding reasons why he or she deserves to survive more than the others. They must always use the first person – "I". The situation and what is at stake are also indicated on the card. There must be complete silence during this first ten-minute phase.

1.   The students work in groups of four to six.

   Each group decides who should be saved according to arguments put forward by each student. To increase interaction, each person must not only defend his or her character but should also attack another. A collective decision must, however, be reached within twenty minutes.

2.   Each group reports their choices and compares with the other groups.

3.   The whole class identifies the values and prejudices that have arisen.

Materials

Some examples of different characters

A 35-year-old decorator, single, who is active in a political movement.	A gypsy who has just come out of prison.
An HIV-positive prostitute.	An old woman, a widow, who is travelling to her native country with her savings in order to see her son again.
A Russian pianist, father of two children.	An English skinhead who is drunk.
A 15-year-old teenager, winner of an important literature award.	An old famous American baseball player.
An ambassador working for the United Nations.	A young mother who has a broken leg.
A soldier coming back from time off-duty.	

Exercise 2.2. – Value systems

Educational objective	The students discover that different values are a possible source of conflict.
Resources	Paper and pens, a worksheet containing a list of different values.

Procedure

A list of 20 values, not in any particular order, is given to each student: social success, love, obedience, security, peace, order, human dignity, feeling good about oneself, equality, respect for others, honesty, family, solidarity, responsibility, justice, tolerance, freedom, competition, health, patriotism.

1. The students work in pairs.

2. The teacher asks the students to group the values on the list in three categories. "In the first, put those that seem most important to you; in the second, the least important; and finally those that are unclassifiable." This work should be done slowly and with thought.

3. Feedback takes place in groups of alternating pairs, by discussion.

   No hierarchy is preferable to another. No assessment or mark will be given for the activity.

   The teacher should emphasise the difference between simple ideal values and effective values – those that take account of a type of behaviour.

4. Ask the students to keep their list with their first choices.

Extension

1. The students form groups of three and compare their respective systems (list of first choice) by answering the following questions:

   – Why have I chosen this value as being the most important?

   – Is this value of any importance for my practical behaviour?

   – What are the obstacles to its realisation?

   – What is my main conflict?

   – What can I do to resolve it?

   – Which are the individualistic attitudes as opposed to genuine collective commitments?

2. The students group their values under categories, for example general ethics or human rights, practical use, general or social success.

   Which grouping seems to be the most significant?

   When faced with a choice, an individual can act unthinkingly according to habit or look for what seem to be the best reasons for acting. We think about values when we ask ourselves not what the best means of reaching a goal are, but which goal should be chosen.

3. This process offers an acceptable solution for all parties confronted with opposing arguments when there is a conflict of interests. Although we are often tempted to use moral terms to defend personal interests, certain principles are in operation. Respect for the individual is a principle, a rule that makes the acceptance or refusal of a category of actions possible.

   The most reliable criterion for knowing whether a rule of conduct favours respect for the individual is reversibility. It makes us give as much weight to the interests of others as to our own.

In groups, students should formulate a few principles such as:

– the law must always be respected

– everyone has the right to live their lives as they see fit.

They can then identify the points of view expressed and the principles.

Exercise 2.3. – Philosophy of life

Educational objective	The students understand that values have different practical implications.
Resources	A list of different ways of life on a poster or on the blackboard.

Procedure

1.   The students assess each "way of life" with the help of the following scale:

   7 – you like it very much

   6 – you like it

   5 – you quite like it

   4 – you are indifferent to it

   3 – you don't care for it

   2 – you don't like it

   1 – you don't like it at all.

2.   The teacher asks the students to compare their rating in pairs or in groups of three or four.

Extension

The students write a description of their ideal way of life (they should try to avoid describing their own present way of life). They find out what the contradictions are; do they conform to their scale of values?

Materials
(see next page)

Different ways of life

1. The following are needed in life: moderation, intelligence, balancing of extremes, friendships, self-control, discipline, foresight, good manners and respect for certain traditions.

2. What counts in life are individual and intellectual freedom, indifference to the material and physical world.

3. The most important attributes are affection, love, devotion, control of one's passions and interests, openness to others. Bold intellects, quest for power and egotism are to be mistrusted.

4. Enjoying life is more important than changing the world: a refusal of ethics, discipline and personal sacrifice; the need for sociability but with periods of solitude.

5. One should identify with a group and seek comradeship. Sociability and action are important, as is a refusal of meditation as an abstraction, of solitude and material interests. Positive emotional externalisation and shared pleasures are preferable.

6. One should seek exuberant physical activity, exploration of one's world and practical senses, a preference for work, the refusal of dreams as nostalgia, the rejection of comfort and self-satisfaction.

7. The days follow each other but they are all different. Instability and adaptation are central, and one should desire to enjoy every important moment. Above all, do not be the slave of an idea.

8. Simple pleasures are important: comfort, friendship, rest, good health, refusal of intense, complex pleasures, rejection of ambition and fanaticism.

9. Openness and receptivity are necessary: pleasures and successes will come on their own; wait calmly and receptively.

10. One must have self-control, but be vigilant, aware of the forces of the world and of human limitations. One must be generous, but not utopian, and go through the world with self-control and dignity.

11. Contemplation is important. The world is too big and too aggressive. The inner life of the soul is essential and has priority over a futile, painful world that must be rejected.

12. The focus is on action, execution, challenge, construction; the body, the hands, the muscles are the true life. Prudence, comfort and relaxation must be rejected.

13. Human beings exist to serve: being useful to others to foster their personal growth. Abandon oneself to the world; be humble, constant, faithful, flexible. Receive without asking, work for the reign of the Good.

Chapter 3 – Getting to know human rights

Introduction

The illustration shows a series of objects that are familiar to children and young people. Each may be read as a symbol of a human right or child's right – a tent (leisure), an umbrella (protection), a plate with food (physical needs), a book (education, freedom of thought), a teddy bear (leisure and play), a flag (protection of citizen's rights by the state), a first aid kit (medical care), an envelope (freedom of communication and expression), a house (privacy). The globe may stand for the idea of protecting human rights for every human being. The symbols are arranged, playfully, above each other, and we may imagine them spinning around. In this way, they are linked to form a whole that adds up to and means more than its parts. Take out one piece, and the whole structure will collapse.

This picture is an example that shows how powerful seemingly simple symbols can be. Finding symbols for human rights is an exercise that can be given to very young pupils, as well as older students too, naturally. It allows them to link their personal experience to human rights and to explore the significance of human rights for their lives, and several of the exercises in this chapter follow this approach.

The exercises in this chapter address human rights – the core topic of human rights education. Other chapters, such as the one on values, emphasise teaching through human rights – with human rights as a pedagogical guideline. These exercises focus on teaching about human rights:

- knowing human rights: the students know one, or several of the human rights in detail and understand the basic principles;

- reading human rights – slowly and carefully, as every word matters;

- linking human rights to everyday life; the students view their personal experience and their wants and needs through a human rights perspective.

This is an approach that is suitable for students of any age.

Several exercises are examples of task-based learning. The students produce a poster or a treasure box and create symbols that stand for certain human rights. By appealing to the students' creative skills, such exercises provide a change from the standard text-based approach.

All exercises require careful reflection in class. The students should understand that human rights may be violated, and therefore need to be protected by laws and means of enforcement (police, a system of punishment).

With older students it is possible to take some further steps. Human rights are fundamental rights, which means no authority needs to grant these rights or is in a position to take them away from us. The students need to know about the existence of the basic human rights treaties such as the European Convention on Human Rights. They need to understand that our rights have limits that are set by the rights of others. We need to find out for ourselves how to do this and, if necessary, legislators and judges will have to decide. As reports by the Council of Europe or non-governmental organisations (NGOs) show, the state itself can also be a threat to human rights. In such cases, citizens may appeal to their national constitutional courts or to the European Court of Human Rights in Strasbourg.

Exercise 3.1. – The human rights poster

Educational objectives	The students understand the following aspects of human rights: their basic structure (who enjoys a human right – content – means of enforcement); the problem of violating human rights; means of protecting human rights.
	The students practise their reading skills.
	The students develop their creative skills.
Resources	Large sheets of paper, A4 size paper in a variety of colours, felt pens, scissors, glue, old magazines and newspapers, pictures and photographs; text of the European Convention on Human Rights or the Universal Declaration of Human Rights.

Procedure

1.   The students form groups of four.

2.   The teacher assigns one article representing a human right to each group. Older students can decide which article they wish to deal with and explain their choice (see step 4).

3.   Each group prepares a poster on a human right. The poster consists of the following parts:

a. the title giving the human right;

b. the text from the European Convention on Human Rights or the Universal Declaration of Human Rights;

c. a picture symbolising the human right (e.g. a car may stand for freedom of movement or a closed front door could stand for privacy);

d. an analysis of the structure of the human right (for advanced classes), referring to:

– the persons who enjoy this right;

– the contents (what the right protects or grants);

– the means of implementation or enforcement;[3]

e. a symbol (e.g. a wheel for freedom of movement or lips for freedom of expression.

4.   The groups present and discuss their posters in class.

Extension

The poster can also contain examples of violations of the human right in question and how it can, or should, be enforced.

Variation

As indicated above, the structure of the poster can be varied according to the age group and the students' knowledge of human rights. The exercise may serve as an introduction or as an application.

When set for advanced classes, the exercise could include aspects such as the type of human right (granting an individual liberty, protecting equality, granting social rights). These could be related to the "generations" of human rights.

---

3. See Yves Lador, *Teaching Guide to the European Convention on Human Rights*, Geneva/Strasbourg, 1997, p. 53f (how is a human right created?).

Used on its own, this exercise could lead to an isolated academic approach focusing on a single human right. It is therefore recommended to combine this exercise with others that refer to the human rights process, for example the students' personal experience, issues of violation and implementation of a human right and discussion on the universal nature of human rights.

Exercise 3.2. – The strings

Educational objective	The purpose of this exercise is to present a global perspective of our common origin and common home as an introduction to human rights education. All people share the same origin, the same earth and they have the same rights regardless of where they live or in what situation. This exercise visualises large figures to make them more apprehensible for children.
Note on method	This exercise stands out in so far as it gives a model of a lecture by the teacher, rather than group work.
Resources	Two pieces of string, 4.8 and 6.7 metres long, preferably a world map or a globe.

Procedure

1. The teacher shows the students the 4.8 metre string and lets them guess how long it is. When the students have agreed that it is 4.8 metres long, she asks them how many millimetres this is.

2. 4 800 millimetres can symbolise the history of our earth, since it is supposed to be 4 800 million years old.

3. The teacher goes back to the creation of the planet and goes through the main events of the earth's history, 1 millimetre being 1 million years. How long have human beings been on this earth? She/he shows them the last 1-2 millimetres and compares it to the rest of the string. Maybe human beings are not that important? Perhaps we should be very careful to take care of the planet we live on?

4. The teacher tells the students a little bit about the history of man. As far as we know human beings originated in Africa. In the beginning, we were all Africans! Then man migrated from Africa and eventually populated the whole earth. Today we are many countries and many different groups, speaking many different languages and having different religions and cultures, but originally we were all the same.

5. The teacher shows the students the second string. How long is it? Today we are 6.7 billion people on earth.[4] Thus 1 millimetre on the string corresponds to 1 million people. She shows the size of some of the larger countries on the string. What is the size of our country? Some people seem to divide the world into "our people" and "foreigners". The string shows us that most people are "foreigners"! But we all share this planet as our home and we have to learn how to live together on it. The countries of the world, through the United Nations Organisation, have decided that even if we are different and live in different places, we all have the same rights.

Extension

From this introduction the teacher can go on to discuss environmental questions, human rights in general, prejudice and stereotypes (see the chapter "Perceiving others"), geographical questions and international relations.

---

4. The teacher should update this figure if necessary and adapt the length of the string accordingly; 6.7 billion was true at the time this book went to print (2008).

Exercise 3.3. – The human rights tree

Educational objective	The students develop a conceptual framework to judge human rights.
Resources	Coloured pens, large sheets of paper to put on the wall.

Procedure

1. The teacher divides the students into small groups of three to five people.

2. He/she asks them to draw a nice tree and call it "our human rights tree". Near the bottom of the trunk of the tree they should write "human rights".

3. Then the tree should have some main branches with some of the key concepts the students think are, or should be, included in human rights. Around these main branches there can be a number of smaller branches with things they think are connected to the main ones.

4. After a given amount of time the groups put their drawing on the wall and explain to the others what they have written on it. These posters can be left on the wall for some time. They will serve as decorations and can possibly also be used again during later lessons.

Extension

After having learned about the students' ideas about human rights, one can go on to study human rights or children's rights in more detail and find out to what extent the actual rights correspond with what the students have written.

Exercise 3.4. – The balloon ride

Educational objectives	The students become aware of universal values in human rights. They understand that some human rights are implicitly contained in others but, within the system of human rights, it makes a difference if specific human rights are protected or not.
	The students understand that human rights are unalienable, and that the arbitrary abolition of human rights borders on dictatorship.
Note on use	This game can be used as an introduction at the beginning of a lesson sequence on human rights or as a transfer exercise at the end.
Resources	Pens and paper, preferably large sheets to be put on the wall; list of the rights to be thrown away/prioritised.

Procedure

1. The teacher manages the game. The students form groups of five to six people. Each group receives a poster and marker pens. The students draw a hot air balloon above the ocean or the local scenery. The sand ballast sacks symbolising ten human rights are stuck on to the poster (see list below).

2. Now the game begins. The students are to imagine themselves travelling with the "human rights balloon". The balloon starts to sink and the passengers have to drop some ballast to avoid a serious accident.

    The task for the students is to prioritise the human rights represented by the ballast sacks. They will use criteria such as the following. Is one right implicitly contained in another? Is one right of particular importance for democracy, or our personal needs?

3. However, the balloon keeps sinking and more ballast has to be thrown out at regular intervals. The students have to drop more ballast sacks. After four or five sacks have been thrown overboard the balloon reaches the ground safely.

4. Reflection in the plenary round. Each group presents their list to the whole class/group and explains (some of) their priorities. Then the lists can be compared. Are there many differences? There should also be a debriefing about the work in the groups. Was it difficult to agree? Was it difficult to give priority to some human rights rather than to others? Hopefully it can be agreed that all the human rights listed are important but that people might differ in their priorities if they had to choose.

    In a functioning constitution, the abolition of any of these rights would cause serious damage to democracy. Human rights are natural rights and therefore unalienable. The balloon ride was therefore a simulation of a situation that we hope will never happen – the rule of a dictator.

    If the students come to question the rules of the game on these grounds, then its learning objective has been fully achieved.

    It is possible to extend the reflection by examining which of these rights has been included in the country's constitution, and how these rights are protected.

Extension

When the exercise is done with younger students, the pieces of ballast – the rights – should be exchanged with items more familiar to the students, for example "free elections" could be substituted by "toys". In the debriefing, these items could then be linked to children's rights.

Materials

Information

The ballast in the balloon consists of the following rights:

– free elections

– freedom of property

– equality of men and women

– a clean and healthy environment

– access to healthy food and clean water

– the right of education

– freedom of thought, conscience and religion

– clothing and housing for all citizens

– private life without interference

– freedom of movement.

Exercise 3.5. – Wants and needs

Educational objective	The students understand the difference between things they want or would like and what they really need.
Resources	Paper, pens, scissors.

Procedure

1. The teacher asks the students to draw some of the things they think they need on pieces of paper (the teacher may prepare the pieces before the lesson or make the students cut them out themselves). They can make around 8-10 drawings each.

2. When the drawings have been done, the teacher divides the students into groups.

3. Each group then has to agree to put away all but five of the drawings. Only the five most important things should be left on the table. Then the groups explain to each other what they have chosen. Have they all chosen the same?

Extension

The teacher hangs a clothes-line (string) across the classroom and pegs a number of the drawings onto the line. He/she discusses with the class which drawings can be removed, things they do not really need. In the end there should only be five drawings hanging on the line. Can the students agree on which five?

Exercise 3.6. – The treasure box

Educational objectives	This is an exercise for children under six. They understand that children have rights, realise that such rights exist and understand that it is important to respect them.
Resources	The treasure box is an extremely pretty box that the children have decorated and filled themselves (with newspaper articles, UNICEF pictograms illustrating children's rights, dolls and various objects).

Procedure

1. In the beginning, the box contains:

    – two pictograms representing the right to equality and the right of the physically or mentally disabled to assistance;

    – two dolls representing children from Guatemala.

2. By collecting objects representing the rights of the child and putting them into the treasure box, the children understand the importance of these rights. The treasure box project should be continued until the end of primary school.

3. In addition to the class's large treasure box, each student has his or her own little treasure box.

Chapter 4 – Perceiving others

Introduction

The picture shows a girl viewing a boy through a magnifying glass. The image created by the magnifying glass is similar but not identical to the boy in reality. The boy does not know what this image of him looks like. It may be wrong or true, even showing more detail than the boy is aware of or that he would like to expose. They are both smiling, so the differences between perception and reality do not seem to present a problem. The girl is smiling at the image, not the boy himself.

We all direct our magnifying glasses, as it were, at other people and store their images in our minds. We judge people by these mental images. They are the raw material out of which we create stereotypes. We all draw on such simplifications of the complex world that none of us is able to understand fully. If stereotypes turn into prejudices, particularly negative ones, they may sow disruption and hostility in society.

The exercises in this chapter help the students to become aware of their perceptions and prejudices of others, to reflect on them critically and to correct them if necessary. This chapter therefore focuses on the social dimension of democracy and human rights. Our mutual perceptions, prejudices and ways of interacting with each other provide the basis on which democracy and human rights need to be rooted. It is not sufficient to have democracy and human rights laid down as the principles of the government and the constitution; their social and cultural roots are equally important.

Generally, the students should understand the function of stereotypes in reducing the complexity of our societies and the world we live in. They should also understand that stereotypes may be dangerous, sowing the seed for hostility in a society. This may happen particularly when we meet people who are foreign and evoke feelings of fear. Education helps people to identify prejudices and misleading stereotypes and correct them.

Older students may also understand that our perceptions and prejudices ultimately contribute to a culture that either supports, or undermines, democracy and human rights in a community. Literally, democracy begins with me – and you.

Exercise 4.1. – All different, all equal

Educational objectives	The students learn to know and accept each other in a group.
	The students discover what they have in common that they were unaware of.
	The students become aware of attitudes and practices related to difference.
Resources	A piece of chalk or a string to make a line on the ground.

Procedure

1. The teacher calls out a series of characteristics one by one. As soon as it is mentioned, those who recognise that they have the characteristic cross the line.

    Examples: all those who ...

    - are wearing jeans
    - have blue eyes
    - are older
    - have visited other countries in Europe
    - regularly read a newspaper
    - have been subjected to discrimination
    - have homosexual friends
    - have prejudices, etc.

    The students can be asked to suggest characteristics, but the teacher must be aware of what might be sensitive.

2. The students discuss the following issues:

    – Did anyone find themselves in a group with someone with whom they thought they had nothing in common?

    – How does it feel to be part of a large group?

    – How does it feel to be alone?

Variation

As soon as a characteristic is mentioned, students move in the class to form groups composed of people with the same characteristics. They stay together for a moment in order to discuss what they have in common. What they say concerns preferences and behaviour, for example.

Exercice 4.2. – Difference

Educational objectives	The students experience difference and understand that difference is rooted in social structures.
	Experience of difference is crucial in adolescence. Young people want to attract attention, be recognised by adults and respected by other people. An important aspect of forming identity in adolescence is the separation from adults, particularly parents.
	The students understand that there are so many biological differences that no one can identify them all. For example, it is impossible to say that one form of intelligence is superior to another. Differences that matter between people are rooted in society – for example by values, social status or social change. In classes in which students belong to cultural minorities, it is a good opportunity for these students to show them in a non-discriminating context.
Resources	A large sheet of paper.

Procedure

1. The teacher lists as many types of differences between people as possible on a large sheet of paper.

2. The class is divided into four groups. Each team lists a particular type of difference:
    - physical differences
    - psychological differences
    - social differences
    - cultural differences.

3. Assessment: students think about the differences between people:
    - "I realise that I know ...
    - ... but I've learned ...
    - My greatest surprise was ..."

Extension

The teacher explains why human beings are both similar and different.

Students imagine, in writing, two situations in which it is difficult to experience difference. This can then be discussed with the whole class.

Exercise 4.3. – True and false

Educational objectives	The students become aware of the stereotypes in their minds and reflect on them critically. They understand that simplifications and stereotypes help us cope with the complexity of the world in which we live.
	The students develop their abilities to make judgments and decisions. In doing so, they are encouraged to develop a critical attitude.
Resources	The classroom must be cleared of desks and chairs. A "true" and a "false" space are defined in opposite corners of the class.

Procedure

1. The students stand in the middle of the room. The teacher reads a series of true or false statements about women, men, various nationalities, etc.

   Reacting to each statement, the students go to one corner or the other according to what they believe is true or false.

   The students with no opinion stay in the middle.

2. The teacher invites the students to explain their choices.

   The teacher provides the correct answer. It is essential that this step is never omitted.

3. The students respond to the teacher's input. The teacher encourages them to explain how they have perceived others, particularly if these perceptions have been proved incorrect.

Extension

The students analyse the manner in which the media deal with issues related to minorities, gender, violence, etc. They identify examples of stereotypes, prejudice, superficiality or thorough and investigative journalism. The students try to correct information that they believe is wrong or incomplete.

Exercise 4.4. – First impressions

Educational objectives	The students are able to identify stereotypes and become aware of the diversity of impressions and perceptions that people have of each other.
	The students practise active listening and learn respect for others.
Resources	Photographs of people which may evoke different reactions by students are stuck on a large sheet of paper (the teacher should choose characters very different in terms of age, culture, ethnic group, etc.).

Procedure

1. The students form a circle. The teacher gives each student a sheet of paper.

2. The teacher asks each student to look at his/her photo:

    – "I see ..."

    – "I think ..."

    – "I feel ..."

3. The students write their first impression on the bottom of the page. They fold the bottom of the page so as to hide the text and pass the sheet to the person on their left.

4. This continues until all the sheets have gone quickly round the circle.

5. The students compare their first impressions:

    – In what ways were your first impressions different or similar?

    – What struck you at your first impression?

    – Which aspects did you not take any notice of, and why?

    – What did the activity show you about yourself?

Extension

The exercise may be done with a very small number of photos, or even just one photo or ethnographic video. Each student may also be asked to write his/her impressions on a piece of paper.

The teacher can give information about other cultures: food, music, family structure, etc.

Exercise 4.5. – We all have prejudices

Educational objectives	In this exercise, the students question stereotypes and prejudices about other people and minorities. They discover the perceptions of different minorities.
	The students become aware of their limits of tolerance and of their confrontational value systems.
	The students are trained to develop their skills of active listening in seeking an agreement.
Resources	One copy of the activity sheet (the scenario) for each student.

Procedure

1. Each student receives a copy of the scenario and reads it silently.

2. Each person chooses three people with whom he/she would prefer to travel and three more they would rather not travel with.

3. The students form groups of four.
    - They compare their individual choices and respective reasons for their choices.
    - They try to agree on a list with three preferences and three dislikes.
    - They choose a spokesperson for their group.

4. Each group presents its list of preferred and excluded companions to the whole class, giving the reasons for their choices.

5. The teacher encourages a free discussion of experiences, for example:
    - What were the main determining factors?
    - If the group has not agreed on a list of preferences, why not?
    - Which stereotypes does the list of passengers imply?
    - Where do these images come from?
    - How would you feel if no one wanted to share a compartment with you, for example?

Extension

The list may be adapted depending on the age group and the students' social background, but it should include people who represent minorities that are clearly discernible at first sight and others that are not.

Minorities and discrimination can also be studied through literature or history.

Materials
(see next page)

The scenario

You have begun a long train journey which is going to last for several days. You are sharing a sleeping compartment with three other people.

Which of the following passengers would you prefer to share your compartment with?

With which of the passengers would you not want to share your compartment?

– a fat Swiss banker

– an Italian disc jockey who takes drugs

– an African selling exotic articles

– a gypsy who has just come out of prison

– a feminist German rock singer

– a homosexual foreign student

– a young Romanian woman carrying a young child

– an English skinhead who is drunk

– an HIV positive prostitute

– a very poor refugee

– an armed foreign soldier

– a young woman who only speaks French.

Exercise 4.6. – We are all equal, but some are more equal than others

Educational objectives	The students identify and analyse the reasons and motives for discriminating against others.
	This exercise focuses on how socio-economic factors affect the chances of social success.
Resources	Large thick sheets of paper and marker pens.

Procedure

1. The teacher divides the students up into groups no larger than six. The groups must be made up of an even number of students. Each group receives a sheet of paper and a marker.

2. He/she asks one half of the groups to draw a caricature of a social winner, the other half a caricature of a loser.

3. The teacher asks the groups to list the characteristics of their model: socio-economic level, profession, sex, ethnic group, leisure activities, choice of clothing, basic outlook, way of life, type of housing, consumer habits.

4. He/she asks the groups to exchange their drawings and interpret them.

5. The drawings are hung up on the wall. Each group is asked to interpret the drawing they have received to the whole class.

6. The "artists" comment on their intentions. By communicating the ideas behind the drawings and the effect of the drawings on the viewer, the students may be expected to touch on the following questions:

    – What are the main characteristics of success?

    – What are the main characteristics of failure?

    – What are the factors that make the difference between "winners" and "losers"?

    – Are the people represented from certain groups?

    – Do all people have the same chances of success, regardless of their social background?

Extension

What are the reasons for discrimination against, and exclusion of, people who are different because of their culture, origin, sexual behaviour, language, etc?

What are the reasons for inequality among humans? Is equality possible, and desirable, or not?

Exercise 4.7. – The tourists

Educational objectives	This role-play simulates a clash of cultures and allows the students to observe the stereotypes they bring into the role-play. It will help students to become aware of possible conflicts in such situations. The exercise makes the students vary their perspectives, by "putting themselves in other people's shoes".
	The students develop their communicative skills.
Resources	A piece of paper or cardboard, coloured markers; if possible, some tourist equipment, e.g. a camera.

Procedure

Note on method

An ideal arrangement would be to work with two different classes, each with a teacher as their leader. The role of the two teachers is to remind the students of the instructions and characteristics of their respective groups: the "tourists" and the "Xs".

1. The two groups meet in their respective classrooms. They have 15 minutes to create the context in which the action will take place and to prepare their roles.

   The tourists write up information about their country, develop their expectations for the journey and prepare the equipment they will have during their journey, e.g. camera, portable telephone, foreign currency. If the real objects are not at hand, they may be symbolised by drawings.

   The "Xs" define their culture: family structure, economy, type of crafts, clothing, and housing. The "Xs" must be as "primitive" as possible. They give themselves a name.

   The cultural elements must be homogeneous. They can also be symbolised by drawings.

2. This activity may be done in the following class period.

   Two tourists, while shopping for souvenirs and taking pictures, meet members of the "Xs".

   They go back to their group and recount their experience. They describe what they have noticed about the strange culture of the "Xs".

   The "Xs" share their impressions of the first meeting with the tourists, giving their opinion of the tourists' attitude.

3. The tourists invade the land of the "Xs", who do not wish to change their ways.

4. The two groups meet for feedback:
   – How do the tourists feel?
   – How do the "Xs" feel?
   – What do the tourists think of the "Xs"?
   – What do the "Xs" think of the tourists?
   – The tourists explain what they found difficult about the behaviour of the "Xs".
   – The "Xs" explain what they found difficult about the tourists' behaviour.
   – According to the tourists, what could the "Xs" have done to make contact easier?
   – According to the "Xs", what could the tourists have done to be less disturbing?
   – If you had to go back to the "Xs'" country, what should you know or do in order to behave appropriately?

Extension

The students interview members of their community who have visited other countries or invite them to spend a lesson in class in order to share their experience of meeting people with a different cultural background.

Variation

The students imagine an ideal society and indicate the significant changes compared with their own culture.

Exercise 4.8. – Globingo: "A human being is part of the whole world".

Educational objectives	The purpose of this game is to show that a human being is part of the whole world.
Resources	A sheet of bingo squares for each student.
	Question sheet.
	Questions for group discussion.

Procedure

1. The students fill in the squares according to the questions asked. Each square has got two lines: one for a name, one for a country. They should try to find for each square the name of one of their classmates, and the name of the country which fits.

   There are a variety of questions which can be asked. You usually need A to L but you can add different ones, though students are only allowed to use the name of a classmate once. Otherwise they have to cross out one square and can't get a "bingo" in that row.

2. After the game, there could be a group discussion. The students will find out that migration is something normal in just about every family and nation. They will talk about global situations and the world as a network.

Materials for teachers

Questions: find someone in the room who ...

– has travelled to some foreign country

– has got a pen pal in another country

– is learning a foreign language

– has got a relative in a foreign country

– enjoys music from a foreign country

– has helped a visitor from a foreign country

– enjoys eating food from a foreign country

– has a car made in a foreign country

– lives in a home where more than one language is spoken

– has got a relative who was born in another country

– has seen a story about another country in the newspaper recently

– has recently talked to someone who has lived in another country

– has learned something about another country on TV recently.

Questions for group discussion

1. What did you learn about one another in this process?

2. What was the most surprising thing you learned about your fellow students?

3. What does the game tell you about our world?

Materials for students: Bingo Sheet

A name: _____ country: _____	B name: _____ country: _____	C name: _____ country: _____	D name: _____ country: _____
E name: _____ country: _____	F name: _____ country: _____	G name: _____ country: _____	H name: _____ country: _____
I name: _____ country: _____	J name: _____ country: _____	K name: _____ country: _____	L name: _____ country: _____

Chapter 5 – Making justice work

Introduction

The picture shows a boy and a girl on a see-saw. The fulcrum supporting the see-saw is not in the middle, providing the girl with a longer lever and the boy with a shorter one. So the girl is dominating the game and she seems to be enjoying it. The boy, with an unhappy look on his face, is trying hard to get down, but his efforts are in vain. Such situations often lead to quarrel and conflict. The fulcrum in the middle carries the symbol of a paragraph referring to the law.

The picture may be read in different ways and it leads to interesting questions. The boy's and the girl's opportunities in this situation are unequal, which addresses the issue of gender equality. Surprisingly, it is the girl who has "the long end" of the stick. Perhaps the girl is cheating, which means she has broken the law, or she is enjoying an advantage granted by the law to overcompensate discrimination against women and girls in the past. So is this a fair game? Is equality always fair? Whose human rights are protected by the law? Are anybody's human rights being violated – and by whom?

The paragraph symbol opens up a further perspective. Who has made the rules of this game? The official symbol of the law refers to the state and the rule of law. The state may consist of institutions sharing power and controlling each other in a system of checks and balances – parliament, government and law courts. It may be run by a benevolent or despotic autocrat. Laws are crucial, as they transform human rights into civil rights for the citizens of a nation state. Laws therefore protect human rights if they are violated. As the picture shows, however, human rights may be violated by fellow citizens or even by an unfair law itself.

Alternatively, the law must strike a balance between the rights of the individual citizens and define the limits of an individual's human rights to protect the rights of others.

The exercises in this chapter address these issues of fairness and justice. The students will realise that justice is crucial for peace and security in society.

Exercise 5.1. – It's not fair

Educational objective	The students become aware of their concepts of justice and injustice.
Resources	Social studies, languages.

Procedure

The students work in pairs.

1. The teacher asks each pair to choose a photo.

2. The teacher asks the students to describe the situation as they understand it:
    – "I can see ..." (factual description)
    – "I feel ..." (affective reaction)
    – "It makes me think of ..." (associations, ideas)

    The teacher then asks them to classify the pictures, using three categories:
    – The photos show a situation which is fair and just.
    – The photos show the opposite, i.e. an example of injustice.
    – The students are not sure how to classify the photos.

3. The pairs form groups of four. Each pair explains their picture to the other pair and should try to convince them of the judgment they have made. The pictures with the groups' comments are displayed in the classroom. Each student should have time to study the exhibits.

4. Plenary session:
    – Which kinds of situations have been described as just – or as unjust?
    – It was difficult to reach a decision on some situations depicted. Why?
    – Which conditions produce injustice?
    – How might these unjust situations be changed?

Extension

The students form several groups. Each group chooses an example of injustice and deals with the last question: How might this form of injustice be overcome?

First, they could identify the human rights which are violated in the case under discussion. Second, they could look for ways to protect and enforce human rights.

Exercise 5.2. – The exception

Educational objective	The students are introduced to the topic of discrimination.
Resources	Different numbers of coloured stickers, and one white sticker.

Procedure

The students work in pairs.

1.   The teacher attaches a sticker to each student's forehead. The students must not know which colour they have. They should therefore close their eyes when receiving their sticker.

2.   The students open their eyes. Each student must now find the other members of his or her group, with the groups finally formed by their colours.

3.   Plenary feedback and reflection. Questions and inputs such as the following are suggested:
     – How did you feel when you met the first person wearing a sticker identical to yours?
     – How did the person wearing the single white sticker feel?
     – Did you try to help each other in your group?
     – How can the person wearing the white sticker be integrated?

4.   The exercise may serve to introduce the students to the relationship between majority and minority groups in society:
     – Who are the exceptions, the excluded ones, in society?
     – Can being the exception, or marginal, be a personal choice?

Extension

The exercise may be taken further by giving advantages to one group. The students may be more involved, but this arrangement might also generate stress and hostility. The teacher should know the class well and must be prepared to react appropriately.

Exercice 5.3. – The jigsaw puzzle

Educational objectives	The game simulates an experience of unfair treatment.
	The students become aware of their reactions to unfair treatment, which are based on ethical principles of justice. Justice is a fundamental category of human rights.
	The students realise the importance of solidarity and co-operation in overcoming injustice.
Resources	Envelopes with simple jigsaw puzzles, or pictures which have been cut up into a few pieces.

Procedure

1. Preparation: there should be a puzzle for every group of three or four students in the class. Teachers can use simple ready-made jigsaw puzzles or prepare such puzzles by cutting pictures (e.g. postcards or advertisements) into a few pieces. Each puzzle should be put into an envelope. Ideally, a duplicate of the picture should be stuck onto the envelope. The teacher takes a part out of some puzzles and exchanges some parts among other puzzles. A few puzzles should be complete.

2. The students form groups of approximately four members. The teacher assigns a specific task to each team member:

    – a student in charge of time and resources

    – an arbitrator who prevents conflict and ensures that instructions are properly carried out

    – a student who has the duplicate of the finished puzzle

    – a student who carries out the task.

    The teacher hands out an envelope to each group, giving them the task to solve the puzzle within a (tight) time limit. The students will quickly discover if their puzzle works out or not and whether they can obtain support from other groups.

3. The game produces clear winners and losers. Depending on the age group and the students' reaction, questions such as the following may serve to articulate and evaluate the experience of positive or negative discrimination:

    – How did you feel when you realised that the groups had different material?

    – How would you have felt if you had been in a different group?

    – How did you feel as part of the group which had too little/too much material?

    – What kinds of behaviour helped, or hindered, a group's success?

Extension

The students are encouraged to discuss real situations in which people do not have equal access to important resources (e.g. disposable time, jobs, money, power).

Exercise 5.4. – The role of law

Educational objectives	Ancient philosophers have drawn on different values in defining the purpose of law.
	The different value options are related to different social and political systems.
	Theory provides a framework for the reflection of daily experience, in which our value options are guided by our interests.
	The students are encouraged to make deliberate choices of values within the framework of human rights, to expose them to comparison and discussion and to be committed to them in everyday life.
Resources	Different concepts of the role of law are written on a large sheet of paper and displayed on the wall (see M 1 in materials section).

Procedure

1. The students form groups of three or four and are given worksheets with a list of rules of conduct (see M 2 in materials section).

2. Each group has to relate the rules of conduct to the underlying concept of law (10 minutes).

3. The groups check their results.

4. The students choose the concept to which they subscribe most.

5. The students choose the concept to which they subscribe least.

Extension

Reflection in class:

- Do the rules you apply in your own life correspond to your choice?
- Do you know of rules which come under the options you have rejected? Have you opposed them? Why? What did you do?

Reflection in writing:

- To which concept of the law are you committed most and why?
- State five rules of everyday life that you adhere to.

Materials
(see next page)

M 1: Basic concepts of law

1. The purpose of the law is to prevent individuals from infringing on other people's rights (Aristotle).

2. The purpose of the law is to give each person what he deserves (Aristotle).

3. The purpose of the law is to create a perfect society (Plato).

4. The law serves to prevent the damage done to individuals by injustice (Glaucon).

5. The law should serve to preserve the interests of those who govern (Thrasymachus).

6. The role of the law is to maintain social peace by ensuring the well-being of all and to enforce the practice of that which is useful for society (Protagoras).

7. The purpose of the law is to protect the weakest.

M 2: Rules

1. People who have brutalised their children will be imprisoned.

2. The state will guarantee the unemployed an income which allows them to survive.

3. Priority for jobs will go to the students who have the best grades.

4. All workers will have to contribute something from their earnings to meet the needs of the unemployed.

5. Any action by one person which causes another person damage will oblige the former to compensate for that action.

6. Teachers will make sure that students know that the laws of our society, being the best laws, are inviolable.

7. Any person who demonstrates his opposition to the organisation of society will be interned in a centre for re-education.

8. Only activities allowed by the state for the well-being of all are authorised.

9. Only taxpayers will have the right to vote.

10. All young people will have to belong to state organisations so that they can engage in useful work.

11. Companies should install anti-pollution filters on chimneys.

12. Nobody will be allowed to disseminate ideas which have not been recognised as valid by the government.

13. The state has the right to expropriate if necessary for the public interest.

14. Company directors have the right to organise private security services.

15. It is forbidden to enter another person's home without his or her permission.

Exercise 5.5. – Perspectives on justice

Educational objectives	The students understand that there can be different perspectives on issues of justice.
	The students develop an understanding of the balance between rights and duties.
Resources	Sets of worksheets containing perspective A or B.

Procedure

1. One of the rights to be examined is chosen.

2. The class divides into groups of four or six.

    One half of each group receives sheet A, the other half sheet B.

    Each subgroup prepares as many arguments as possible in defence of the statement figuring on their sheet.

3. The groups reunite. The members of subgroup A present their point of view to the members of subgroup B, who must listen attentively and take notes.

    Then it is subgroup B's turn.

    The presentation of arguments may be followed by a period during which the members of the different subgroups ask each other questions.

4. Subgroups A and B exchange roles. They must not be informed in advance of this part of the exercise.

    They are given a few minutes to reconsider their arguments.

5. The groups attempt to adopt a common position in writing on the problem under debate.

6. Questions to consider:

    – Which difficulties did you encounter in trying to reach a common position?

    – Did the fact that you reversed roles make it easier or more difficult for you to agree on a common position?

Extension

The teacher (or students) find cases in which freedom of expression (or child labour) is a controversial subject.

    – How can rights and duties be balanced?

    – Are there duties – or rights – which impose limits on certain rights?

Information given in the media should be used for the case studies. The investigation could be extended to include other human rights, e.g. freedom of movement or the right of property.

Materials
(see next page)

Perspective A: Freedom of expression

In a fair society freedom of expression is a fundamental human right that should not be restricted. Consider the following points:

- the negative effects of censorship;
- the political implications of its limitation and of dissidence;
- the circumstances in which other countries restrict it;
- the importance of freedom of expression for democracies;
- any other relevant problem.

Perspective A: Child labour

Laws against child labour should be strictly applied so that the right of children to play, to learn and to become healthy adults is protected. Consider the following points:

- the lack of education which follows when children are obliged to work;
- the fact that children often work in unhealthy conditions;
- the way child labour is often exploited because children are not organised to protest against unjust treatment;
- any other relevant problem.

Perspective B: Freedom of expression

In a fair society it is sometimes necessary to restrict freedom of expression in order to protect people's rights. Consider the following points:

- the effects of racist remarks on minorities;
- the ways in which speech may be used to encourage violence;
- how in some countries freedom of expression is unrestricted and leads to the violation of rights;
- the need to promote duties as well as rights;
- any other relevant problem.

Perspective B: Child labour

In the interests of helping families to survive in difficult economic circumstances, and of helping children to assume an active role in society, children should be able to work and help support their families. Consider the following points:

- the fact that in some societies where employment is rare, children can be one of the only sources of income a family has;
- the fact that in many societies children traditionally worked longer than adults;
- the opinion that preventing children from engaging in productive work results in useless isolation of children from the world of adults;
- the fact that work can be a formative experience for children;
- any other relevant problem.

Chapter 6 –
Understanding political philosophy

Introduction

The picture shows a boy and a girl facing each other. They are showing each other a cube with symbols that stand for political philosophies. It is important that they are smiling at each other, as the symbols differ and indicate controversy and disagreement. It is worth while exploring the meaning of the symbols, as far as this is possible. The boy shows the "ban the bomb" symbol, confessing to pacifism. The pentagram could stand for a Socialist point of view, but also for a holistic view of humankind in the universe. The zigzag lines may stand for water, as a symbol for protection of the environment, but the meaning could also be completely different. The girl shows the A-symbol of anarchism. The female gender symbol might stand for a feminist viewpoint. The flower could stand for the protection of the environment, or peace, but the girl may also have given this symbol a different meaning. The young people are making use of human rights – freedom of thought, freedom of expression and equality. There is no authority to decide who is right and who is wrong.

The picture carries an interesting and surprisingly complex message. We combine symbols and concepts in political philosophy to express our ideas and views, but they may be ambivalent or misleading. Therefore we must explain our choices to each other and we must listen carefully. There are many points on which we can agree or disagree. The six symbols suffice to give us an idea of an open, pluralistic society. We should treat each other with respect; then we can have a good argument that harms no one and benefits everyone.

Education for democratic citizenship and human rights (EDC/HRE) integrates two dimensions. The first is related to *content*. Understanding political philosophy is important in EDC/HRE, as it provides us with a sense of direction and values when we judge issues and take action. We also understand others better.

The second dimension of EDC/HRE refers to the *culture* of civilised conflict – arguing with a smile, if possible. Such a culture of conflict must be taught in school, by experience and reflection. This can begin at an early age and a lot depends on the example set by teachers and principals. The EDC/HRE teacher should take care to avoid two pitfalls. One is political correctness. It is not the teacher's task to teach the students any preferred political doctrine, nor should he/she press them to accept his/her personal views. The second is silent neglect, which is a subtle form of oppression. Students should learn to expect and grant mutual attention and response. The teacher should encourage the students to explain their choices so that others can understand them, but they should not be pressed to justify them.

The exercises can be adapted to different age groups and may be used from elementary to upper secondary level.

Exercise 6.1. – Basic concepts of political thought

Educational objectives	The students understand the values that implicitly guide political argument and debate and that some of these values support human rights, while others oppose them (teaching *about* human rights).
	The exercise trains students to be willing to study and understand values and attitudes regardless as to whether they agree with them or not (teaching *through* human rights).
Resources	A list of propositions or slogans (see materials below). Alternatively, election posters, video clips or excerpts from statements or speeches in political life could be used.

Procedure

1. The students form pairs or groups of four.

2. They identify the implications of the statements. It may be necessary to provide them with questions to guide them and allow a comparison, e.g. for which groups in society a proposal may have implications and what these implications might be (the students would find answers such as the rich and the poor, the healthy and the sick, the powerful and the weak, etc.).

3. If they have already been introduced to basic approaches of political thought, the students could link the proposals to the different schools of thought. They may find affinities to more than one line of thinking.

4. The students judge the statements and their underlying values in the light of human rights.

Extension

The students discuss the implications of the propositions by relating them to issues under discussion in their country.

Materials

List of propositions and slogans

1. The state should not interfere with the management of the economy. It should limit itself to enforcing the law.

2. Free medical care should be guaranteed.

3. All companies should be nationalised.

4. The head of state should be accorded full powers.

5. The state, the employers and the unions should meet to determine the rate of increase in wages.

6. The state in itself is a nuisance.

7. White civilisation is the superior civilisation.

8. Weak students should be prevented from slowing down others in their studies.

9. Nobody has the right to give other people orders.

10. Society should be organised so that the ruling order respects the natural hierarchy of things.

Exercise 6.2. – Attitudes to power[5]

Educational objectives	The students can distinguish between concepts of power and their implications for democracy and human rights.
	The students develop active listening (teaching *through* human rights).
Resources	Set of student handouts: "Statements on power and government".

Procedure

1. The students form pairs. They study the statements and decide which statements they are in agreement with.

2. They make notes of the reasons why they support a certain statement.

3. The pairs present their results in class.

4. The students identify the underlying schools of political thought (transfer exercise); the teacher uses the findings and discussion in class to introduce the students to (selected) approaches of political thought (inductive approach, allowing different methods to be used – lecture by the teacher and perhaps the students; study of excerpts).

Extension

The students reflect on their individual value systems.

The students relate political ideas to the policies of parties and political leaders in their country.

Materials
(see next page)

---

5. Adapted from Claude Paris, *Ethique et Politique*, Editions C.G., Québec, 1985.

Student handout

Statements on power and government

1. In a government the role of the leader is paramount and irreplaceable.

2. Power alienates and must be eliminated in order to allow each person to realise his full potential.

3. A nation has only one dangerous enemy: its government.

4. Political power should be exercised by people chosen by the citizens.

5. Political parties are detrimental to the power of the state because they divide the people and cause futile confrontation.

6. The state is not a simple collection of individuals; it is a reality higher and more essential than the sum of individuals.

7. All forms of power have a tendency to become totalitarian.

8. The state is not an end in itself but the means necessary for the realisation of individual aspirations.

9. The state is an immense cemetery where all expressions of individual life end.

10. Strikes are a challenge to authority, which is why they should be forbidden.

11. Individuals exist only for the state and are nothing outside it.

12. Young people should take part in the decisions that concern them.

13. Only when the state has ceased to exist will we be able to talk of freedom.

14. The teacher should take the legitimate claims of his/her students into account.

15. Human beings have a natural tendency to do good; we should always have confidence in them.

16. The participation of all individuals in power should be a fundamental principle of the organisation of all human communities.

17. Political parties make it possible for the aspirations of citizens to influence the decisions of government.

18. Left to themselves without any control, human beings would kill one another.

19. Political power should not be at the mercy of public opinion.

20. Human beings have rights that power should respect and promote.

Exercise 6.3. – If I were a magician

Educational objectives	The students are encouraged to create meaningful visions. A person without utopian visions is confined to accepting the status quo.
	The students are given the chance to use their talents (creativity).
Resources	Paper and a marker pen.

Procedure

1. The students are asked to imagine themselves in the role of a magician.

2. They read:

    "If I were a great magician, I would arrange for men, women and children never again to live through what happened during the war, and for this to happen ..."

    Each student completes the following sentences:

    – I would stop ...

    – I would close ...

    – I would forget ...

    – I would oppose ...

    – I would continue ...

    – I would create ...

3. In turn, the students read out their answers in a plenary session. It is suggested that the chairs are arranged in a circle.

4. Evaluation: the students point out and discuss which desires and needs they have discovered.

Extension

The students deal with the question as to whether anything could be done to make one of their wishes come true.

Variation

For older students:

"If I were an architect ...": the students imagine what their school, or the town or city they live in, could or should look like.

The students can reflect on their wishes and relate them to basic traditions of political thought (Liberal, Conservative, Socialist, Friends of the Earth).

Chapter 7 – Taking part in politics

Introduction

The picture shows a man and a woman, supported by a girl and a boy, advocating their causes in public. The man's poster shows the globe as a symbol of the world, while the woman is drawing attention to the five-pointed star on her poster, held by the boy supporting her. Perhaps this symbol corresponds to the surface they are standing on. Their expressions are friendly, there is no sign of hostility. Adults and children are taking part in politics. They are making use of their right to demonstrate peacefully in public. Both sides are mixed in gender, therefore no gender issue is at stake. The two groups are competing – for attention and support by the majority. They are in direct confrontation, so no media, political parties or interest groups are involved.

The four people are standing on a surface resembling an irregularly pointed star. This symbol may be read in different ways. It may stand for the community that gives its citizens a sense of belonging together and that also provides a framework for rights, responsibilities and duties. The star could also resemble "the floor" that a citizen takes when speaking in public. Whoever chooses to stay off this floor will not be heard and must accept the decisions that are finally made. Citizens can take part in politics in many ways. EDC/HRE focuses on ways of active, direct participation. Taking part in politics is a right of children, not only of adults. To do so requires an understanding of the issue and careful judgment. Political participation in democracy needs to be taught in schools, which in turn requires schools to function as micro-societies that give students the opportunity to participate in managing their school affairs.

Both in democratic schools and democratic society, argument and controversy, even quarrel and conflict, are nothing to be feared but should be seen as something normal, even useful in democratic decision making. Settling clashes of ideas and interests are the basic method of solving problems and making decisions. If interests and objections are not articulated, they cannot be taken into account. In an open society, harmony – the "common good" – cannot be imposed, but needs to be negotiated. Controversy and conflict are not harmful if set in and supported by a culture of argument, conflict resolution and compromise.

The exercises focus on framework conditions and modes of political participation. This helps the students to appreciate their opportunities to participate in their community.

Exercise 7.1. – The wall of silence

Educational objective	The students become aware of their concepts of democracy.
Resources	Pieces of flipchart paper fixed to the wall and markers (for groups of five).

Procedure

1.   The students form groups of five. Each group is seated in a semi-circle facing a flipchart fixed to the wall. They are asked to write, in silence and within a time limit, a sentence of the type: "Democracy is ..."

2.   The students respond to sentences or words already written down.

3.   After the time limit for writing on the poster has been reached, each student chooses and reads out a sentence he/she has not written him/herself. The students share their results in class.

4.   Thoughts are shared:

   – "I have learnt ..."

   – "I have discovered ..."

   – "I would like to discuss ..."

Variation

Instead of using posters on the wall, the students sit round a table writing on a large sheet of paper.

General information

"The wall of silence" is a brainstorming method that may be used at the beginning of a lesson sequence on key concepts such as democracy, dictatorship, justice, peace, education, equality, liberty, etc.

The method supports students who are less extrovert or wish to take some time to think carefully before saying something. Often these students are at a disadvantage in standard, that is oral and frontal class settings.

Exercise 7.2. – My feelings about dictatorship

Educational objectives	The students can define and judge elements of democracy and dictatorship.
	The students can make a deliberate choice of values and argue for them.
Resources	Poster and markers or blackboard and chalk.

Procedure

1. The students are asked to define the characteristic traits of dictatorship.

    The list might contain points such as the following:

– anti-Semitism	– the role of women as reproducers
– ethnic cleansing	– repression of sexual minorities
– torture	– submission to authority
– conditioning	– pressure from peers to conform
– the cult of power, individuals or the military	– the demand to be led
– view of criticism as destructive	– rejection of minorities

2. Referring to the list, the students try to answer the question, "To what extent does this situation affect me?"

3. The students are asked to place these items on a scale, starting with the trait they feel strongest about.

Extension and variation

The features of dictatorship can be related to examples from news reports, films or textbooks.

The same exercise could be done on democracy.

Exercise 7.3. – Questionnaire on attitudes to change

Educational objectives	The students can reflect their personal attitudes and express them freely.
	The students can listen to other students, regardless of whether they agree with each other or not.
Resources	Set of student handouts: "Questionnaire on attitudes to change".

Note for the teacher

Information on basic political attitudes

An *attitude* is a tendency to express an opinion or adopt a certain form of behaviour. It results from social integration and personal history and is therefore less conscious than ideology. Attitudes guide our perceptions, our judgments and our actions.

The purpose of the exercise is to see, on the basis of the expression of opinions, to what extent a person is, or is not, in favour of social change. Change in itself is neither a good nor a bad thing, and the purpose is not to pass judgment on the students, much less to evaluate them. It should also be borne in mind that the results of such a "political litmus test" should not be taken too seriously, particularly if the students are not fully aware of the implications involved in a statement in the questionnaire.

The real question is: why, what, when and how to change. The models of political thought serving as guidelines for political attitudes have developed since the era of the French and American revolutions. The following sketch can serve as a rough guideline but cannot replace the reading of the original sources.

A *progressive* attitude leads to a belief that changes are desirable. It may be revolutionary or *reformist*, depending on the perceived urgency and on the means employed. For the *revolutionary*, if necessary, even violence is not ruled out. For a reformist too, change is desirable, but without radical rupture with the past.

A *conservative* attitude, on the other hand, values tradition and prefers experience to theory. It may favour the status quo or be reactionary. To favour the status quo means to hold that although it is imperfect, the present state is acceptable. Organic growth may be advocated as the mode of change (Edmund Burke). A fundamental concern is to keep the state strong and agile lest it be overburdened by partial interests and excessive participation. The reactionary, however, refuses the present state of things: he/she holds that it was a mistake to carry out changes in the first place and wishes to return to an earlier state.

The *revolutionary* and the *reactionary* tend to be doctrinaire, that is, fundamentalist, which means that they defend a position on an ideological basis, without taking present reality into account.

The others are more pragmatic and define their positions by an analysis of immediate consequences.

This exercise may serve as a rough guideline to make students realise the existence of different models of political thinking and to become aware of their personal preferences and leanings. In political life, political attitudes will often be found to resemble a policy mix between different basic models of political thinking, for example when arguing along neo-liberal, ecologist, or technocrat lines.

Procedure

1. The students answer the questions. Before each statement they write a number to indicate their attitude. The code they use is as follows:

    5 – They are fully in favour of the statement.

    4 – They are more or less in favour of the opinion stated.

    3 – They are more or less neutral regarding the opinion stated.

    2 – They are more or less against the opinion.

    1 – They are fully against the statement.

2. Students draw up their total, which indicates their political attitude.

    100-80: revolutionary

    80-60: reformist

    60-40: in favour of the status quo

    40-20: reactionary.

Are there any revealing divergences between students, notably between boys and girls?

Extension

Working with texts: depending on how this exercise is used – as an introduction or a transfer exercise – text work is recommended to precede or follow this exercise. For advanced classes, excerpts from writers such as Locke, Burke or Marx might be selected. In addition, or as an alternative for younger students, statements by politicians or party representatives on a specific issue may be appropriate.

Also see the following exercise.

Variation

These questions may be formulated on the basis of more local concerns.

Any of the questions may serve as a starting point for debate.

Materials
(see next page)

Student handout

Questionnaire on attitudes to change

1. A woman should be able to get sterilisation without the permission of her husband.

2. Information on birth control should be available on request to all young girls of fourteen or over.

3. Soft drugs should be legalised.

4. In democracies referenda should be possible on popular demand.

5. Criminals need medical care rather than punishment.

6. The death sentence should be completely abolished.

7. Big companies should be nationalised.

8. Marriages between people of the same sex should be legal.

9. There should be no specification of sex in job offers.

10. Charitable institutions should be banned. It is the duty of the state to help the underprivileged.

11. The average individual does not need to be managed or controlled.

12. Students should take part in the running of their school.

13. Grades and certificates should be abolished.

14. Everyone should be guaranteed a minimum income, regardless of sex, age and profession, and even if they decide to do nothing.

15. Children should be brought up in several faiths simultaneously; they can make their choice when they are adults.

16. Political leaders should follow the advice of scientists on the use of scientific discoveries.

17. Human beings are all born with the same potential.

18. Private property should be banned and state property brought in.

19. Nobody has the right to impose their opinions on others.

20. All production of polluting products has to be prevented, whatever the immediate economic impact.

Exercise 7.4. – The planning project[6]

Educational objectives	The students understand the structures of mutual dependence in a community during a period of change.
	The students understand that every decision concerns all members in the community. If a decision is therefore to be accepted and supported, all members of a community must understand it and have the chance to participate in the decision-making process.
Resources	A description of a real or fictional planning project of an urban neighbourhood. It has to take into account social, economic, demographic, transportation and other problems.
	The teacher needs to prepare a set of cards for the actors in the role-play. The following examples may serve to give the reader an idea of how a real planning project could be simulated in a role-play.

Note for the teacher

There are many goals hidden inside this exercise. It is up to the teacher to decide which of these elements should be explicitly discussed and which should just help the teacher to understand and explain to others what the potential learning effect could be.

1. The students develop the willingness to listen to, and understand, different points of view and interests, whether they agree with them or not.

2. The students learn to anticipate the consequences and implications of options in the decision-making process.

3. The students experience decision making in a democratic framework. This needs to find a balance between participation and efficiency (e.g. everyone should have a say, but there needs to be a time limit for each contribution and the process as a whole).

4. Basic insight: in an open, i.e. learning community, the common good (the *volonté générale*) is not defined by any authority but is agreed on in a temporary decision which is open for revision if new problems occur.

Procedure

1. The students divide into pairs. Each pair receives a copy of the project and one of the cards. One pair of students presides over the debate to follow.

2. The pairs establish a list of all the benefits and problems relating to the project.

3. They do so from the point of view of the person whose role they are playing.

4. They take a common decision for or against the project (15 minutes).

5. In turn, each pair presents its position to the group and explains its reasons.

6. In a debate, each pair has to say what it would like to see carried out. A time limit should be set for each student and the whole debate.

7. The students vote so as to decide whether the project will be implemented or not.

Follow-up work

8. Are there other groups whose opinions should be consulted?

9. To what extent was your opinion influenced by that of others?

---

6. Adapted from S. Fountain, *Education pour le développement humain*, De Boeck, 1996.

10.   Do the particular interests defended by one of the groups have an effect on the other groups?

11.   Are there groups whose opinions and interests deserve more weight?

12.   Are there groups whose opinions are rarely or never heard?

13.   Does the solution which the majority has voted for represent the best solution for the whole of the society?

Extension

1.   Individual students act a certain role without the support of a partner.

2.   The role-play includes the hearing of experts who can refer to specific aspects of the project.

3.   Part of the class acts as a jury or local parliament who make the final decision, without the advocates for certain interest groups participating (representative democracy).

4.   Two or three students act as reporters and observers. They feed back on the process of decision making and the roles played by the students.

5.   If a real decision-making process is simulated in a role-play, local politicians or journalists can be invited to a follow-up discussion with the students.

6.   This model may be used to organise a real decision-making process in school.

Material for the teachers

Questions for designing role-play cards

1. You are a teacher:
    – Do you see reasons why the project would be a good idea?
    – Do you think it could present any problems?

2. You are the owner of a small business:
    – Do you see reasons why the project would be a good idea?
    – Do you think it could present any problems?

3. You work in a medical centre.

4. You work as a refuse collector.

5. You are a bus driver.

6. You are a recent arrival from another region or another country and are seeking work.

7. You are young people working in the neighbourhood.

8. You are the manager of a small company.

9. You are a political representative.

10. Etc.

Exercise 7.5. – We and the world

Educational objectives	The students examine how other countries and remote events affect their community.
	The students understand better the structure of interdependence in the world.
	The unequal distribution of power and the unequal process of development call for worldwide understanding and co-operation in the spirit of human rights.
Resources	Current local newspapers, a map of the world, tape and coloured markers, thread, needles.

Procedure

1. The students form groups of four. They cut out articles which show that another part of the world has an effect on their local community and that their country and other countries mutually affect one another.

2. The issues:
    - economic problems
    - political problems
    - problems of migration
    - pollution
    - cultural exchange
    - tourism
    - military action, etc.

3. The students classify articles according to keywords which they choose to indicate certain types of influence and attribute colours to the keywords.

4. The students choose the most significant articles and tape them onto the map of the world on the wall. They trace lines linking each article with thread and needles to their country.

5. Plenary session.
    - What part of the world have you established most links with?
    - What kinds of links are most common? Why?
    - Is there a part of the world with which you find no links? Why?

Extension

The students find information about the political and/or economic systems in force in the countries with which there are links.

They can see whether other links existed in the past.

In foreign language teaching, materials from foreign newspapers or the Internet can be used.

This exercise may serve as an introduction to the problem of unequal development and power distribution in the world.

Our perception of the world we live in is fed by information we receive second-hand – from the media. Just think how far you would get if you only knew those parts of the world around you that you've seen yourself. So what do the media tell us and what information don't they pass on to us? Should anyone control the media? A censor? Or is competition between different newspapers enough? How powerful are the media? Could we live without them? Other similar questions can also be raised but the students should raise them, not the teacher. If the students realise how limited their scope of direct perception is, they may begin to ask questions on the role of the media by themselves.

Exercise 7.6. – Should we take part in politics?

Educational objectives	The students form their opinions as to whether it is important to participate in government.
	Participation can take place in many ways. We define participation as taking part in the public life of your community and society. Some people think it is important to participate, while others do not. The students should understand that political decisions affect them, regardless of whether they participate in decision making or not.
Resources	Role cards for the role-play.

Procedure

1. Four students role-play the conversation between some newly arrived citizens in a nation in the process of creation.

2. The students discuss, guided by the teacher if necessary, questions raised by the role-play such as the following:

    - What are the four main views expressed by the citizens about participation? Do you agree? Why or why not?

    - What will the four citizens lose by not participating? What benefits do you think individuals will gain from participating?

    - What benefits do you think the new country would gain from individuals participating?

    - What are the possible risks or losses involved if one chooses to participate?

    - Weighing benefits and risks, do you think it is worthwhile participating?

3. By discussion or lecture, the students could arrive at the following conclusion:

    Government affects people's lives in lot of ways. By participating in government people can have a voice in decisions made by the government. In every society someone is going to make the decisions. If people choose not to participate, they will not have a say in those decisions. These decisions can include such things as:

    - how much people will have to pay in taxes;

    - whether the society will get involved in a war;

    - who is going to own and control the country's natural resources.

    Depending on how the government is structured, decisions can be made at different levels, including national, regional and local. Some decisions, such as those about military power, are often made nationally, while others, such as those concerning transport and roads, are often made regionally. Still others, such as those about rubbish collection, are frequently made locally.

Materials
(see next page)

Role-play: four citizens arrive in a newly formed country

Assume you have just arrived in a newly formed country. You are eager to get started, to get to work building a new society. You have heard that there are all kinds of possibilities to create good government. Then you overhear the following conversation among a group of your fellow new arrivals:

Citizen 1:

"Where I came from, no one cared much about politics and government. We were always too busy with our daily lives. So here I probably won't want to bother about politics either."

Citizen 2:

"That's the way it is in our country ... and I never really understood what was going on among the leaders. They made it seem so complicated and made it very easy for us not to bother trying to understand."

Citizen 3:

"Well, it was different in our country. We tried but people who had power wouldn't let us get involved and we were threatened if we did try. So finally we gave up trying to participate."

Citizen 4:

"In my country we had elections and our leaders promised us good government. But it never turned out that way. The leaders used government to get rich. All leaders are corrupt."

Exercise 7.7. – How does government affect your life?

Educational objectives	The students understand that government affects our lives in almost every aspect imaginable (*tua res agitur*). The world we live in is man-made and it is up to us what we do with it.
	Deliberate political decision making is necessary because of our ever-increasing dependence on one another, from local to global level.
	Democracy can best take into account competing interests and integrate them into a satisfactory compromise – provided all groups have been given a hearing.
Resources	None.

Procedure

1. The students should realise to what extent their lives are affected by government. The following questions are suggested to help them; they could be answered in class or in small groups which would then present their results in the plenary setting.

2. – Tell the story of a recent day in your life – where you went, what you wore, saw, ate, said, learned and did. List whether each thing that you mentioned was affected by government, including national, regional and/or local government.

    – Assume that your government is a democracy where all citizens are given an equal opportunity to participate without their human rights being violated. Which of the items in your daily life that you listed as being affected by government do you think would have to change? Explain why you think they should change.

3. The students will probably raise the question as to how people can participate in democratic government. The teacher should offer some information, either through a lecture or based on a textbook or worksheets.

    The result could be as follows: many people believe that the greatest opportunity to participate in government is offered in a free and open democracy. This type of government means that the people themselves gain power and govern usually through the rule of the majority. Some countries are democracies in name only and people are not really allowed to participate. In a democratic system, citizens can choose between different ways of participating and some may even decide not to participate at all.

    Democracy can best take into account differing and competing interests and search for satisfactory solutions – provided all sides have articulated their points of view. Special attention must be paid to weaker groups, who are not in a position to exercise pressure and whose interests therefore tend to be ignored (problem of exclusion).

Exercise 7.8. – Ways of participating in democracy

Educational objective	The students relate different forms of political participation to human rights.
Resources	List of possible forms of political participation.

Procedure

1.   Each student writes a list of all the ways and activities by which he or she thinks people can participate in democratic decision-making processes.

2.   The students form groups of four. They compare their lists, discuss them and try to agree on one list of ways of participating.

3.   The groups compare their list of ways of participation with the one on the handout.

Extension

The students could explore the following questions:

1.   Do you believe that any or all of the above forms of political participation are human rights? Should all of them be protected by the law? Explain why or why not.

2.   In what way can you participate in democracy in your country? Are there any ways of taking part that are not open to you? Explain.

3.   Should laws also protect the right not to participate? Explain.

Materials

Student handout

Participation may take many forms including:
- reading about issues and leaders
- writing about issues and leaders
- debating issues
- working in the community in support of a particular cause or in protest against government action
- forming or joining political parties or other community or grass-roots organisations
- attending political or community meetings
- becoming a leader of a political party, a labour organisation or community organisation
- voting in elections
- campaigning for those standing for office
- standing for office and serving if elected
- paying taxes
- lobbying
- serving in the military
- using existing legal channels such as contacting government officials, taking cases to court, etc.
- protesting through demonstrations, boycotts, strikes, etc.

Exercise 7.9. – The policy cycle

Educational objectives	The students are able to apply the model of the policy cycle to examples of decision-making processes.
	The students become aware of their opportunities in intervening and participating in processes of decision making.
Resources	Set of student handouts: "The policy cycle model".
	Flipchart paper, markers, scissors, glue.

Procedure

1. The teacher introduces the model of the policy cycle, using one of the following approaches:

    – The teacher employs the deductive, systematic approach: he/she gives a lecture[7] and the students apply the tool that they have been given.

    – The teacher follows the inductive approach: the teacher begins with an example or refers to knowledge and experience that the students already have. This could be a current issue, a decision that they support or disagree with or a problem that they are worried about. A decision in school can also serve as a starting point. The teacher follows with a lecture, carefully referring to the context provided by the students.

    Whatever approach is used, the students receive a copy of the handout "The policy cycle model".

2. The students apply the model. Different tasks can be given:

    – The students use the model as a tool for active and structured reading of the newspaper. Working in groups of four to six, the students study the newspapers of the past few days and identify examples for each of the six stages. They paste the articles on their posters and present them in the plenary round.

    – The students follow a decision-making process on a particular issue. This may require material covering a longer period of time and therefore older newspapers can be useful too. Books and the Internet can become important sources. This exercise can be developed into a research project.

3. The model can serve as a starting point for discussion: in what stages of a decision-making process can we intervene? The teacher should explain that the two stages "decision" and "implementation" are confined to the political system (unless a decision is made by plebiscite). But citizens may intervene in any other stage.

---

7. See "background information for teachers" (in the material section of this exercise).

Materials

The policy cycle model: Politics as a process of problem solving

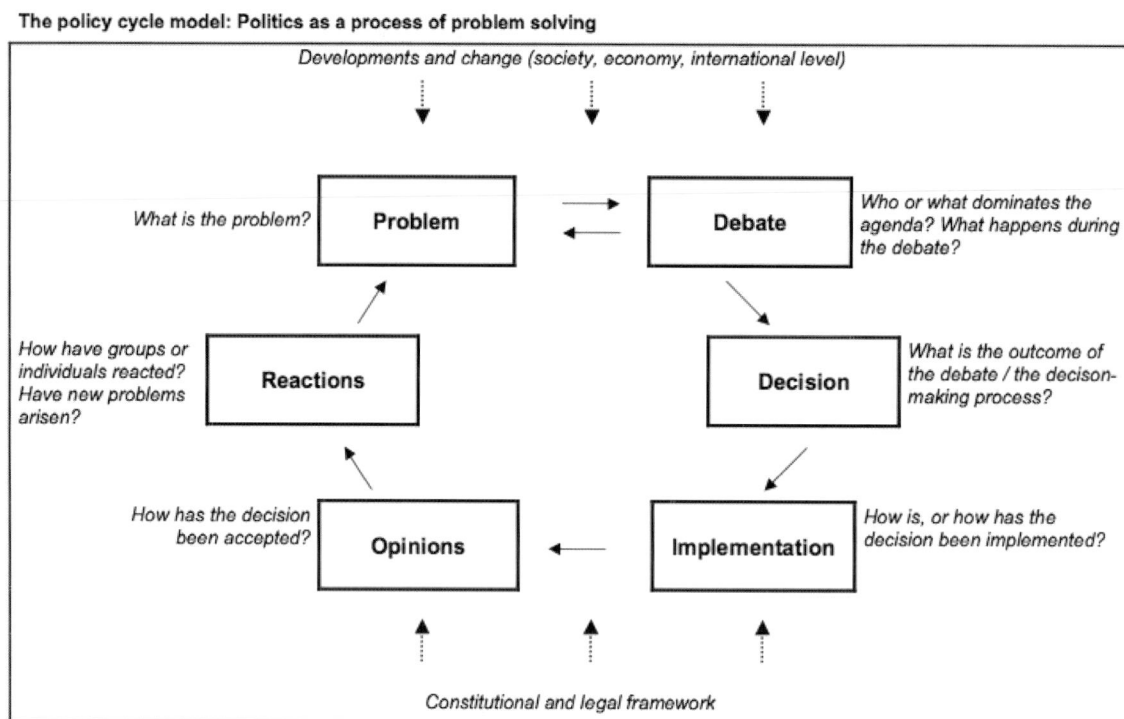

Developments and change (society, economy, international level)

What is the problem?	**Problem**	**Debate**	*Who or what dominates the agenda? What happens during the debate?*
How have groups or individuals reacted? Have new problems arisen?	**Reactions**	**Decision**	*What is the outcome of the debate / the decision-making process?*
How has the decision been accepted?	**Opinions**	**Implementation**	*How is, or how has the decision been implemented?*

Constitutional and legal framework

The policy cycle model: background information for teachers

The policy cycle is a model. It works like a map, which means it selects certain aspects from reality and ignores others. In this way the picture becomes clearer but the user should never confuse the model with reality. In this case, the policy cycle model focuses on politics as a process of decision making and solving of problems. Its focus is not on politics as a struggle for power, even though this aspect does appear. The six categories lead to key questions that help to analyse political decision making; the students are encouraged to develop further questions that are more context-specific.

The model gives an ideal type description of political decision-making processes. First, a political *problem* must reach the public agenda. The issue of agenda-setting has a lot to do with political power. Problems do not exist as such; they must be defined and accepted. Competing interests and values play an important part, as the definition of a problem strongly influences the outcome of decision making. For example, poverty can be defined as an attack on human rights or as an incentive to take one's fate into one's own hands. The first view implies that poor people need support, while the second view tacitly recommends not helping poor people too much, as this might make them lazy. The key issue of agenda-setting is indicated by the double arrows between the categories *problem* and *debate*.

The *debate* takes place under certain conditions. The frame of the model is important here: social, economic and international developments set the data. And the constitutional and legal framework defines the rules. Who may take part in the debate? Who decides what? These questions help to understand the outcome of the debate, the final decision. Who took part in the debate? What interests were at stake? What had to be negotiated? Was it possible to find a compromise?

Implementation: How is, or how has the decision been implemented? Did any difficulties or conflicts occur? Does the implementation meet the intentions of the decision makers?

Opinions: How did the decision "go down"? Whose interests are affected – favourably or unfavourably? What values are involved?

Reactions: Are there reactions by individuals and/or collective, organised reactions by groups? Do they support or oppose the decision? Examples could be protests, demonstrations, letters to the editor of a newspaper, decisions by a court, strikes, emigration, withdrawal of investors, breaking the law, etc.

Problem: At the end of the day, has the original problem been solved? Have any undesired or unforeseen effects been produced? Has a new problem arisen through the reactions to the decision and its implementation? The policy cycle is terminated if the problem has been solved. Very often, a new cycle begins with a new subsequent or unforeseen problem.

The students should understand that the policy cycle shows where and how citizens can take part in politics. We can give our definition of problems that need political attention and require public resources to solve them. We can take part in the debate, form our opinion on the decision and support or oppose the way in which it has been implemented. In doing so, we are making use of our human and civil rights. Democracy depends on active democrats.

Chapter 8 – Dealing with conflict

Introduction

The illustration shows two young men engaged in a quarrel. They are sitting opposite each other at a table. One is waving a flag, the other is clenching his fist, baring his teeth. Their hair is raised, which gives the opponents a fierce, beast-like look. If this was all, then we would expect this conflict to escalate: the two men would soon get up and resort to physical violence. But there is a second element in the picture: the two men are shaking hands, as a sign of agreement and compromise. They are only talking – perhaps shouting at each other – but there is no violence.

The picture shows simultaneously what takes place successively in real life: if we stand up for our interests, opinions and values, we will sometimes get involved in conflict. To resolve such conflicts, we must be able and willing to find an agreement and also strike a compromise. Arguing first and marking the extremes, and then looking for an agreement and compromise, comprises a process of conflict like breathing in and breathing out.

The star-shaped floor may also be meaningful. We share one community – for example our planet, our family, our school. We have no other. Therefore we depend on each other and carrying out conflicts and resolving them must be governed by shared principles and rules. Conflict as such is nothing bad. Human rights produce a pluralism and competition of interests, which increases the likelihood of conflict. Good conflict resolution can lead to harmony, while the attempt to suppress conflict by authoritarian means or resolve it unfairly can lead to the disruption of a community.

Conflict resolution is, to a certain extent, a skill that can be taught. This is one focus of the exercises in this chapter; they provide the learner with tools, structured schemes of procedure, for conflict resolution and mediation. Secondly, fairness of conflict resolution is important, and this refers to the values and the culture of conflict behaviour. Ideally, a conflict should be overcome by a win-win situation. If that is not possible, care must be taken not to produce losers, but rather to find a compromise that maintains a balance in sharing benefits and disadvantages. Viewed from a wider perspective, the potential stakeholders include not only the opponents who are directly involved, but also the community and the environment as a whole.

Exercise 8.1. – Win–win solutions

Educational objective	The students understand that a conflict can be resolved in different ways. The parties involved may be in the position of winners or losers, or may both have agreed to a compromise. No party should feel that they are a loser, as this may well lead to a new outbreak of conflict.
Resources	Blackboard or flipchart.

Procedure

1. The teacher explains to the students that there can be three different types of solution to a conflict:

win – win	☺☺
win – lose	☺☹
lose – lose	☹☹

   He/she illustrates these principles of conflict resolution on the blackboard or a flipchart.

   Win-win: solutions which allow both parties to benefit

   Win-lose: solutions in which only one party benefits at the expense of the other

   Lose-lose: solutions in which neither party benefits.

2. The teacher gives examples of the different ways of conflict resolution:

   A boy and a girl are quarrelling over a ball. An adult intervenes and makes them play together with the ball or gives them equal time to use it. They both benefit. If the adult gives the ball just to one of them, of course only one benefits. If the adult takes the ball away, since the children cannot agree, neither benefits.

3. In pairs or in groups the students explore their personal experience to find further examples of conflict. They may discuss their experience of conflict at home and at school and may move on to the larger conflicts involving groups of people and whole states.

4. The students analyse examples of conflict resolution, identifying them using the model presented above, asking which party will benefit from the solution. Who can find solutions that allow all/both parties to benefit?

5. Plenary session: students share the results of their analysis.

Variation

After step 2, the students receive a case description of a conflict. In groups, they try to find a solution that avoids producing losers. If the conflict already has been resolved, the students can compare their solution with the one found in practice and the reactions that followed. This analysis follows the policy cycle model (see exercise 7.9).

Exercise 8.2. – A structured approach to conflict resolution

Educational objective	The students learn a technique of conflict resolution. They understand that resolving conflicts depends to a certain degree on skills that can be learned.
Resources	Set of student handouts: "Resolution of conflicts in six stages". Newspapers and magazines.

Procedure

1. The teacher describes a situation of conflict to which there is no defined solution (example: one student makes fun of another student who comes from a foreign country and speaks with a strong accent).

   The situation may be presented by a role-play. The students discuss how to resolve the conflict. In doing so, they may anticipate parts of the model they will use in this lesson or ask questions that the model may provide an answer for.

2. The worksheet "Resolution of conflicts in six stages" is distributed to half the students, who study it in silence.

   The other half of the class selects a report on a conflict from a newspaper or magazine. They may also draw on personal experience or first-hand knowledge.

3. The students form groups of four consisting of two students who have read the resolution of problems and two who have defined possible conflicts.

4. The students choose one conflict and test the ideas of conflict resolution.

   Two are adversaries, the other two act as mediators, using the sheet to find a solution.

5. Follow-up plenary session:
   – Which conflicts did you try to solve?
   – How did you try to solve them?
   – (How) did the model of conflict resolution help you?

Variation

1. The students focus on a case study and compare their solutions.

2. Once students are familiar with the procedure it can be applied to conflicts actually occurring in class.

Materials
(see next page)

Student handout: resolution of conflicts in six stages

1. Identify needs. "What do you need (what exactly do you want?)"	Each person involved in the conflict should answer this question without accusing or blaming the other.
2. Define the problem. "What do you believe to be the problem in this case?"	The whole class can help to find an answer which meets the needs of those concerned. The adversaries must be able to accept the definition.
3. Seek a number of solutions. "Who can think of a possible way of solving the problem?"	All members of the class can contribute answers. These should be written down, without comment, judgment, or evaluation. The aim at this stage is to produce as many solutions as possible.
4. Evaluate solutions. "Would you be pleased with this solution?"	Each party in the conflict reviews the alternatives, explaining which are, or are not, acceptable.
5. Decide which solution is best. "Do you both accept this solution? Has the problem been solved?"	It must be clear that both parties accept the solution. Their efforts to find a solution should be appreciated.
6. See how the solution is applied. "Let us talk once more about this situation and make sure that the problem really has been solved."	A plan should be set up to evaluate the solution. Depending on the nature of the conflict and the age of the adversaries, an evaluation may be carried out minutes or hours or a day later.

Exercise 8.3. – Family and peer conflict

Educational objective	The students learn about solving conflicts in a structured manner.
Resources	Set of student handouts: "Resolution of conflicts in six stages" (see Exercise 8.2).

Procedure

1. The students read the worksheet "Resolution of conflicts in six stages".

2. The teacher lets the students come forward with examples of typical conflicts at home, in school or in the playground, for example:

    At home:
    - The child wants to play, but the parents think he or she should study.
    - The child wants money for the cinema / a concert / a party / a picnic, but the parents have other expenses to take care of.

    In the playground:
    - Boys and girls want to use the playground for different purposes.
    - Boys disturb girls while they are playing.

3. The students choose one conflict to work on and form groups of four to six.

4. Each group then divides into two, half of them taking the role of parents and half the role of children (or boys/girls).

    First parents and children come together separately to work out their position. Then they meet with their opponents and start negotiations following the six stages.

    After a given time negotiations stop and the groups get back into class.

5. The whole class feed back on their work in groups. What kind of solutions did they arrive at? Were there many different solutions?

Variation

This exercise could also be done with a mediator, for example with one student taking the role of a grandparent who leads the conflicting parties through the negotiations.

Exercise 8.4. – Brainstorming session on conflict and peace

Educational objectives	The students can define the concepts of conflict and peace.
	The students can explain which kinds of conflict can be resolved and which cannot.
Resources	Flipcharts and coloured markers.

Procedure

1. The word "CONFLICT" is written on one of the sheets.

   The students receive two tasks for brainstorming.

   a. They write down as many expressions or words referring to conflict as come to mind.

   b. They add keywords referring to situations of conflict.

   This part is carried out in silence, without commenting.

2. When the students have run out of ideas, the word "PEACE" is written on the other sheet. Same procedure.

3. The class discuss the results.

4. A classification of the different types of conflict is developed with the teacher:

   – conflicts which *can* be resolved

   – conflicts which *cannot* be resolved.

   Conflict resolution without losers (see Exercise 8.1) is very often only possible through compromise. This works, for example, when scarce resources need to be shared fairly. If the cake is small and every eater receives an equally small piece, I can accept the solution even if I stay hungry. But if a clash of values or religious beliefs is involved, compromise is hardly possible. And if a conflict is caused by ethnic or racial divisions, there is the danger of expulsion or physical extermination of the members of one party. The more rational the approach of the parties to a conflict is, the bigger the chance to resolve it by negotiation and compromise rather than by violence. Rational conflict resolution requires the parties to distinguish between the issue and the opponent and to respect the opponent's human dignity in terms of human rights.

Extension

The students illustrate different situations of peace and conflict through drawings or articles and photos from the press.

Exercise 8.5. – The statues

Educational objective	The students are able to identify situations of oppression, to develop creativity in non-violent conflict resolution and to use body language as a means of expression.
Resources	None.

Procedure

1. The students carry out the following preliminary exercises in pairs:

    – One student strikes a pose; the other has to imitate. They reverse roles.

    – One student places his hand a few centimetres from his/her partner's. When he/she moves his/her hand the other has to twist into whatever (uncomfortable) position is necessary to keep the same distance.

    These exercises train students to take notice of each other.

2. In the plenary session, the students represent and discuss situations of oppression:

    – Two or more students agree on an idea and then form a group of statues to represent a situation of oppression (example: a kneeling child polishing the shoes of a seated rich man).

    – If a member of the audience thinks of a way of resolving the situation and making it more equal, he/she rearranges the actors according to his/her new model.

    Ideally the exercise should be conducted in silence, to encourage the students to mime and develop expressiveness.

3. More actors may participate in the scene progressively.

4. The teacher reserves the last 10 to 15 minutes of the lesson for a follow-up plenary session. The students give feedback, and they may come forward with questions that can lead to further study.

Variation

1. The same procedure is used to illustrate human and children's rights and instances of how they are violated.

2. The exercise may be resumed in situations of conflict and in real situations that invoke strong feelings.

Exercise 8.6. – Punishment versus positive conflict resolution

Educational objectives	The students are encouraged to accept the notion of law and of rules in a group.
	The students are able to accept differences and to take part in decision-making processes.
	They develop their creative potential in resolving conflicts.
Resources	Set of student handouts: "List of punishments".

Procedure

1. The students brainstorm forms of punishment. This introduction to the lesson addresses them as experts, as they may draw on experience and observation. They may already add comments.

    The teacher distributes the handout "List of punishments" to the students, and they read it in silence.

2. The students discuss in small groups (three or four) which punishments make sense and which ones do not.

3. The groups share their results with the other groups (the jigsaw arrangement is useful here; see Exercise 5.3).

4. The students return to their groups and discuss which punishment, if any, should be imposed in the following situations:
    – A student arrives late at school.
    – A student has not done his homework.
    – A student disturbs work in class.
    – A student offends a classmate because of his/her ethnic origin or religious beliefs.
    – A male student molests a female student.
    – A student is violent in class/during break.

5. Plenary session: the students present their results.

    The follow-up discussion could deal with the following question: are there any alternatives to imposing a punishment (e.g. mediation between the wrong-doer and the victim)?

Extension

The students act out a scene of positive, creative conflict resolution in class.

Materials
(see next page)

Student handout

List of punishments

1. Writing a poem

2. Telling a fairy tale to little children

3. Presenting jokes and quizzes to the class

4. Ten push-ups for swearing

5. Standing in class after school as many minutes as you came in late in the morning

6. Standing up while writing

7. Preparing a lesson for the class

8. One hour of gardening

9. Cleaning the recreational area

10. Cleaning the classroom

11. To be dismissed from the lesson

12. Running round the school building ten times

13. Detention during break

14. Extra work in one of your weak subjects

15. Payment of a fine which contributes to cover general expenses

16. Writing an excuse

17. Further suggestions ...

Exercise 8.7. – Minorities

Educational objective	The students understand that the sense of exclusion can be the result not only of the way other members of society see you, but also of the way members of your own group see you.
Resources	A set of positive cards and a set of negative cards for each group.
	Two flipchart sheets for each group, one bearing the word "FEELINGS" and the other the word "ACTIONS".
	Marker pens.

Procedure

At the beginning of the game, it is essential that the students have no idea of what they represent, otherwise they might immediately resort to preconceived ideas which would distort the course of the game.

The game is an example of careful and complex framing by the teacher. Within the strict framework, the students have great liberty to develop and express their ideas and experiences.

1.   The students form groups of four to six (preferably not more).

2.   Each group receives a set of positive cards, a marker pen and the two sheets of flipchart paper. The teacher asks them to appoint a writer to record the group's comments and reactions on the flipcharts. Alternatively, all group members record their own reactions.

3.   The teacher tells the students that they will not represent themselves during the exercise, but will act as members of a minority group. For the moment, they should enquire who they are, but also consider the messages on the cards as describing them and their situation.

4.   In turn, the students read one of the cards out to the other members of the group. When they have read all six cards, they write their answers to the question, "How do you feel as a member of this group?" on the "FEELINGS" sheet.

5.   The teacher distributes the six negative cards to each group, and they repeat step 4.

6.   The teacher asks the students to answer the following question, "What would you do if you were in a similar situation?" The answers are to be written on the "ACTIONS" sheet. The students should bear in mind that they are still the same group who expressed their feelings on the first sheet. Perhaps something they have felt or written on that sheet might help them decide how to act.

7.   Plenary session:

 – Each group present their feelings as set out on the sheet headed "FEELINGS" to the rest of the class.

 – When all the groups have completed Part I, the teacher asks them to present their suggestions on their "ACTIONS" sheet. The class should identify constructive actions and acts of violence and differences between and within groups.

8.   The teacher asks the students how they worked in the group and whether they encountered any problems while doing the exercise (co-operation, leadership, etc.), and what they think they have learned from the exercise: about themselves, their reactions and the group. Can they establish a relationship between the minority group which they represented and other groups they might know?

9.   Lastly, the teacher tells the students that the group they represented is the group of Tinkers, otherwise known as Roma or Gypsies.

Extension

The students compare their ideas with the Convention on the Elimination of All Forms of Racial Discrimination.[8] The students can also explore whether the situation described seems to correspond to that in their own country, what measures are taken by the authorities to deal with the problem and which of the measures they have suggested follow the convention.

Materials

Set of positive and negative cards

Our houses are unlike those of other people. They are special and we are very fond of them. We like to keep our traditions.	Television programmes and the press do not tell the truth about us. They say that we are a problem. They do not let us tell our part of the story.
We have many skills. We do all kinds of manual and craft work. Our work is a major contribution to the country we live in.	Some people treat us badly and give us bad names. Sometimes we are attacked without reason. Thousands of our people were murdered abroad, not very long ago.
In the past, our people performed many brave acts. We like to remember our history.	We never have running water, our refuse is rarely collected.
We are very independent. We prefer to look after ourselves. We do not owe anything to anybody.	Some doctors do not want to treat us when we are sick. It is difficult for us to receive social security benefits.
We like getting together and telling stories and singing songs. We think this is very important to enjoy life.	People do not want us in their neighbourhood. Some people do not want to give us a job because of what we are.
We try to live near our family and friends. We look after the old people in our community very well. We adore our children.	Sometimes we have problems with the police and the municipal authorities because of the place we happen to be at.

8. Convention on the Elimination of All Forms of Racial Discrimination, adopted by the UN General Assembly on 20 November 1963. The text is accessible via the Internet.

Exercise 8.8. – Images of war and peace

Educational objectives	The students can define aspects of war and peace.
	The students develop the skill of reading images.
	The students are able to express their personal ideas and feelings about war and peace.
Resources	A pool of pictures (including photos, cartoons, advertisements, etc.).

Procedure

1.   Some photographs are displayed to the students. Ideally the photos are hung up on the wall around the classroom or in a well-lit corridor. The students should be able to view the pictures as in an exhibition.

2.   The students receive the opportunity to react spontaneously. Which images represent peace – or war? The teacher does not press a student to comment. At the end of this introductory step, he/she points out if the students have agreed in their comments or not. Differences of perception are not discussed further.

3.   The students select a photograph that appeals to them particularly. They should be able to view it closely if they wish. In silence, they answer the following questions in writing:

– What do you see (description)?

– What are your thoughts (reflection and imagination)?

– What are your feelings (emotions)?

4.   In groups of four the students select images and form pairs of contrasts. They may include some of the photos they have studied in step 3, but they may also choose other photos.

5.   The students present their selections in the plenary and give reasons for their choice. If time is running out, each group should present at least one pair of contrasts.

6.   Reflection. The students express their feelings and thoughts. They may ask questions about the situations referred to in the photos, and these questions could lead to further study.

Extension

The same subject can be studied in literature and painting.

The class organises an exhibition on the themes.

Illustrations

Introduction

The Swiss artist Peti Wiskemann has created the illustrations for this book. They express the key topics of the exercises by artistic means, thus opening new approaches for the students to understand democratic citizenship and human rights. The following pages contain full-size reproductions of the pictures for copying and presentation in class.

Building up classroom atmosphere

Illustration from Chapter 1

Democracy and Human Rights Education – Volume VI

Teaching democracy
A collection of models for democratic citizenship and human rights education

Clarifying values

Illustration from Chapter 2

Democracy and Human Rights Education – Volume VI

Teaching democracy
A collection of models for democratic citizenship and human rights education

Getting to know human rights

Illustration from Chapter 3

Democracy and Human Rights Education – Volume VI

Teaching democracy
A collection of models for democratic citizenship and human rights education

Perceiving others

Illustration from Chapter 4

Democracy and Human Rights Education – Volume VI

Teaching democracy

A collection of models for democratic citizenship and human rights education

Making justice work

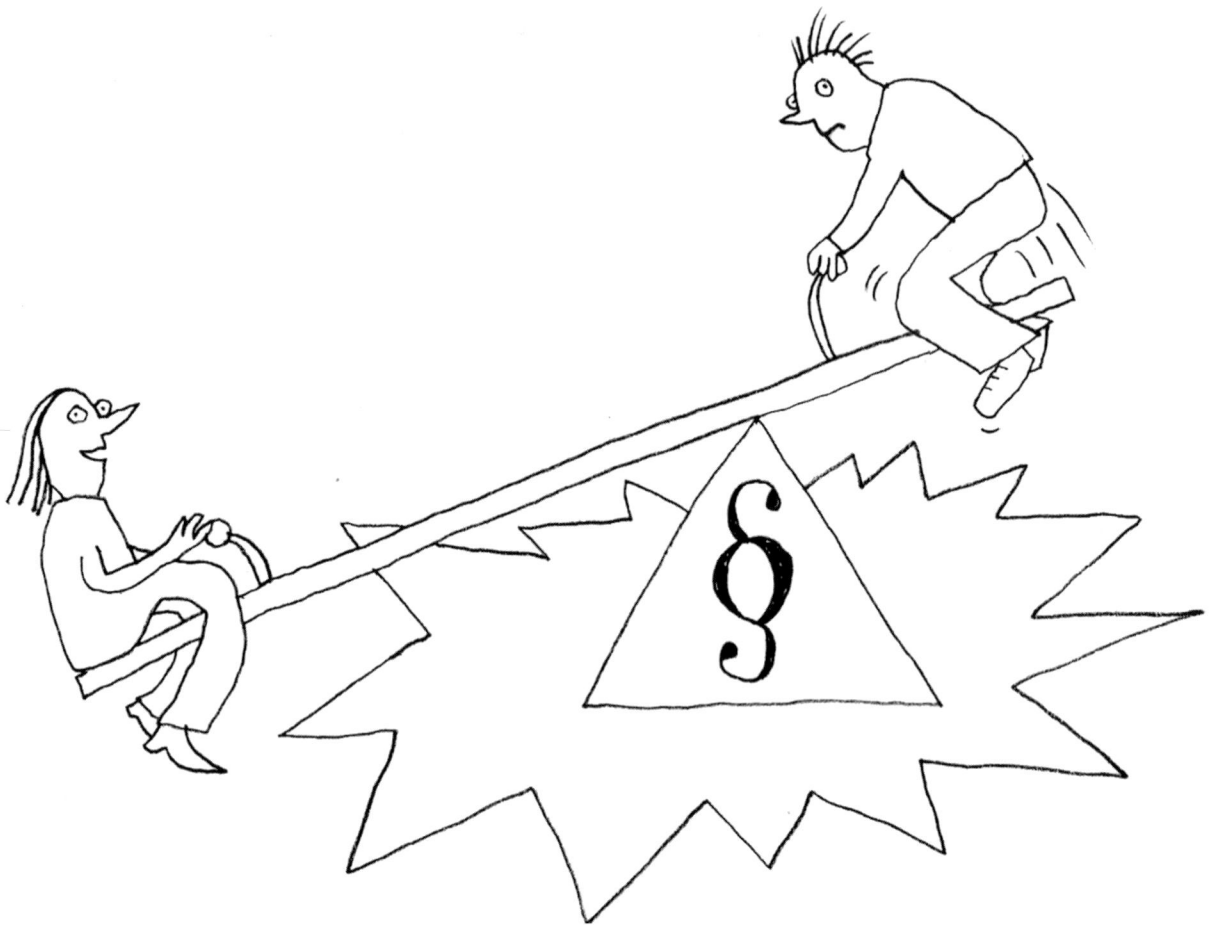

Illustration from Chapter 5

Democracy and Human Rights Education – Volume VI

Teaching democracy

A collection of models for democratic citizenship and human rights education

Understanding political philosophy

Illustration from Chapter 6

Democracy and Human Rights Education – Volume VI

Teaching democracy

A collection of models for democratic citizenship and human rights education

Taking parts in politics

Illustration from Chapter 7

Democracy and Human Rights Education – Volume VI

Teaching democracy

A collection of models for democratic citizenship and human rights education

Dealing with conflict

Illustration from Chapter 8

Democracy and Human Rights Education – Volume VI

Teaching democracy

A collection of models for democratic citizenship and human rights education

BELGIUM/BELGIQUE
La Librairie Européenne -
The European Bookshop
Rue de l'Orme, 1
B-1040 BRUXELLES
Tel.: +32 (0)2 231 04 35
Fax: +32 (0)2 735 08 60
E-mail: order@libeurop.be
http://www.libeurop.be

Jean De Lannoy
Avenue du Roi 202 Koningslaan
B-1190 BRUXELLES
Tel.: +32 (0)2 538 43 08
Fax: +32 (0)2 538 08 41
E-mail: jean.de.lannoy@dl-servi.com
http://www.jean-de-lannoy.be

CANADA
Renouf Publishing Co. Ltd.
1-5369 Canotek Road
OTTAWA, Ontario K1J 9J3, Canada
Tel.: +1 613 745 2665
Fax: +1 613 745 7660
Toll-Free Tel.: (866) 767-6766
E-mail: order.dept@renoufbooks.com
http://www.renoufbooks.com

CZECH REPUBLIC/
RÉPUBLIQUE TCHÈQUE
Suweco CZ, s.r.o.
Klecakova 347
CZ-180 21 PRAHA 9
Tel.: +420 2 424 59 204
Fax: +420 2 848 21 646
E-mail: import@suweco.cz
http://www.suweco.cz

DENMARK/DANEMARK
GAD
Vimmelskaftet 32
DK-1161 KØBENHAVN K
Tel.: +45 77 66 60 00
Fax: +45 77 66 60 01
E-mail: gad@gad.dk
http://www.gad.dk

FINLAND/FINLANDE
Akateeminen Kirjakauppa
PO Box 128
Keskuskatu 1
FIN-00100 HELSINKI
Tel.: +358 (0)9 121 4430
Fax: +358 (0)9 121 4242
E-mail: akatilaus@akateeminen.com
http://www.akateeminen.com

FRANCE
La Documentation française
(diffusion/distribution France entière)
124, rue Henri Barbusse
F-93308 AUBERVILLIERS CEDEX
Tél.: +33 (0)1 40 15 70 00
Fax: +33 (0)1 40 15 68 00
E-mail: commande@ladocumentationfrancaise.fr
http://www.ladocumentationfrancaise.fr

Librairie Kléber
1 rue des Francs Bourgeois
F-67000 STRASBOURG
Tel.: +33 (0)3 88 15 78 88
Fax: +33 (0)3 88 15 78 80
E-mail: francois.wolfermann@librairie-kleber.fr
http://www.librairie-kleber.com

GERMANY/ALLEMAGNE
AUSTRIA/AUTRICHE
UNO Verlag GmbH
August-Bebel-Allee 6
D-53175 BONN
Tel.: +49 (0)228 94 90 20
Fax: +49 (0)228 94 90 222
E-mail: bestellung@uno-verlag.de
http://www.uno-verlag.de

GREECE/GRÈCE
Librairie Kauffmann s.a.
Stadiou 28
GR-105 64 ATHINAI
Tel.: +30 210 32 55 321
Fax.: +30 210 32 30 320
E-mail: ord@otenet.gr
http://www.kauffmann.gr

HUNGARY/HONGRIE
Euro Info Service kft.
1137 Bp. Szent István krt. 12.
H-1137 BUDAPEST
Tel.: +36 (06)1 329 2170
Fax: +36 (06)1 349 2053
E-mail: euroinfo@euroinfo.hu
http://www.euroinfo.hu

ITALY/ITALIE
Licosa SpA
Via Duca di Calabria, 1/1
I-50125 FIRENZE
Tel.: +39 0556 483215
Fax: +39 0556 41257
E-mail: licosa@licosa.com
http://www.licosa.com

MEXICO/MEXIQUE
Mundi-Prensa México, S.A. De C.V.
Río Pánuco, 141 Delegacíon Cuauhtémoc
06500 MÉXICO, D.F.
Tel.: +52 (01)55 55 33 56 58
Fax: +52 (01)55 55 14 67 99
E-mail: mundiprensa@mundiprensa.com.mx
http://www.mundiprensa.com.mx

NETHERLANDS/PAYS-BAS
De Lindeboom Internationale Publicaties b.v.
M.A. de Ruyterstraat 20 A
NL-7482 BZ HAAKSBERGEN
Tel.: +31 (0)53 5740004
Fax: +31 (0)53 5729296
E-mail: books@delindeboom.com
http://www.delindeboom.com

NORWAY/NORVÈGE
Akademika
Postboks 84 Blindern
N-0314 OSLO
Tel.: +47 2 218 8100
Fax: +47 2 218 8103
E-mail: support@akademika.no
http://www.akademika.no

POLAND/POLOGNE
Ars Polona JSC
25 Obroncow Street
PL-03-933 WARSZAWA
Tel.: +48 (0)22 509 86 00
Fax: +48 (0)22 509 86 10
E-mail: arspolona@arspolona.com.pl
http://www.arspolona.com.pl

PORTUGAL
Livraria Portugal
(Dias & Andrade, Lda.)
Rua do Carmo, 70
P-1200-094 LISBOA
Tel.: +351 21 347 42 82 / 85
Fax: +351 21 347 02 64
E-mail: info@livrariaportugal.pt
http://www.livrariaportugal.pt

RUSSIAN FEDERATION/
FÉDÉRATION DE RUSSIE
Ves Mir
9a, Kolpacnhyi per.
RU-101000 MOSCOW
Tel.: +7 (8)495 623 6839
Fax: +7 (8)495 625 4269
E-mail: orders@vesmirbooks.ru
http://www.vesmirbooks.ru

SPAIN/ESPAGNE
Mundi-Prensa Libros, s.a.
Castelló, 37
E-28001 MADRID
Tel.: +34 914 36 37 00
Fax: +34 915 75 39 98
E-mail: libreria@mundiprensa.es
http://www.mundiprensa.com

SWITZERLAND/SUISSE
Van Diermen Editions – ADECO
Chemin du Lacuez 41
CH-1807 BLONAY
Tel.: +41 (0)21 943 26 73
Fax: +41 (0)21 943 36 05
E-mail: info@adeco.org
http://www.adeco.org

UNITED KINGDOM/ROYAUME-UNI
The Stationery Office Ltd
PO Box 29
GB-NORWICH NR3 1GN
Tel.: +44 (0)870 600 5522
Fax: +44 (0)870 600 5533
E-mail: book.enquiries@tso.co.uk
http://www.tsoshop.co.uk

UNITED STATES and CANADA/
ÉTATS-UNIS et CANADA
Manhattan Publishing Company
468 Albany Post Road
CROTON-ON-HUDSON, NY 10520, USA
Tel.: +1 914 271 5194
Fax: +1 914 271 5856
E-mail: Info@manhattanpublishing.com
http://www.manhattanpublishing.com

Council of Europe Publishing/Editions du Conseil de l'Europe
F-67075 Strasbourg Cedex
Tel.: +33 (0)3 88 41 25 81 – Fax: +33 (0)3 88 41 39 10 – E-mail: publishing@coe.int – Website: http://book.coe.int